LOW COMEDY IN DARK THEATERS

BY
CLIFF LEWIS

Copyright © Cliff Lewis, 2018. No part of this book may be reproduced or distributed in any form or by any means, or stored in a data base or retrieval system, without written permission from the author. All rights, including electronic, are reserved by the author.

Printed in the United States of America.

First edition 2018.

Cover image: Carl Grupp, "The Magic Omelet II", lithograph.

Scurfpea Publishing
P.O. Box 46
Sioux Falls, SD 57101
scurfpeapublishing.com
editor@scurfpeapublishing.com

Contents

All Maps Lie	1
Love in the Wet and Dry	2
Bombus Polaris	3
"Supposing Truth..."	4
C'est la vie, c'est la guerre, c'est la pomme de terre	5
Graffiti Reverie	6
Who Are the Pigeons?	8
Panhandle Red Dirt Blues	10
Late Summer Heat	11
Headgear to Heaven	12
One Answer to Nietzsche	14
Black Shoes on the Move	15
Cave! Cave! Deus Videt	16
Gone	17
BeBop, BeBop	18
Behind the Mirror	20
The *David* Forever	21
Syriana	22
The Muffin, Unheated	23
The Last Stop Vinyl Shop – NYC, 1995	24
Ötzi on My Mind	25
The Last Elm	26
That Old Black Magic	27
Two Graves	28
Thoughts to Avoid Late at Night	29
In the Hood	30

Well-Behaved Bacon 32
The Book of Lascaux 33
Falling Down While Sitting in Ecclesiastical Angst 34
By Any Other Name 36
Say Hello to David Hume 38
Double Ditch By the River 39
LOL 40
Got Lakht 42
Just Another Poem About Twinkies® 44
Life in the Lab Fast Lane, 1963 – 69 45
Hopper Here 46
Disconsolate Robin 47
Vacation in the Country 48
1946 49
Black on White 50
Celebrating the 4th at Mount Rushmore 51
Azalea Days 52
Alto Bitter Blues 53
Notes on the Return of LSD in 2017 54
I Repeat 55
On Cranes (Not the Birds) 56
Mud on My Face 57
Love, Incidentally 58
Five Women: Mostly True Love Stories 60
McSonnet 62
Something Says Nothing 63
The Undistorted Communication Game,
    Sans Jürgen Habermas 64
Going to School 65
Over and Out 66
Love Lessons Learned 67
Books 68
Galileo at the Mill 69
Hopes Considered 70

The Cherry Tree 71
One Day Soon 72
Dimethylcadmium 73
Starstruck 74
Negotiating Desire 75
Copernicus at Rest 76
The Waiting Room 77
"From My Cup of Tea" 78
Academic Vaudeville 79
A Crow Bar "True" Story in First Person 80
Horn Island Blues 81
Toxic Principles 82
In the Country, I Note 84
Innovation 85
Laissez Faire 86
Bus Token Taken Without Response 87
At the Faculty Club 88
The Answer to the Old Riddle
    That Cannot Be Asked in Writing 89
Poet's Day Off 90
Scientists At the Wall 91
Optimistic Pessimist 92
Gimme Shelter 93
Photoautotrophs 94
Cycle Interrupted, 1948 95
The Tuned Eye 96
A Sunny Afternoon in April 98
Neither Here Nor There! 100
On the Job 101
Before the Battles 102
Under the Bomb 103
Compulsion to Speak 104
Damsel in Distress 106
The Top at the Bottom 107

Chauvet-Pont-d'Arc	108
Acetylcholinesterase, I Know Thee Well.	110
Doors	112
In the Coop.	113
The Bust of Socrates	114
Around the Stove, 1945	116
'Possum Hunt, 1927	117
It's Just for You	118
Austin, 1972	120
Lost in Translation.	121
Avatar	122
From the Candle's Perspective	124
Apart-ment	125
The Girl in the Green Dress	126
Visit to Good Earth State Park at Blood Run	128
No Remorse in Wyoming	130
In Our Image	131
Better Things for Better Living…Through Chemistry	132
Springtime Not Really So Bad Blues	133
An Icy Winter's Tale	134
Where are the Poets?	135
Just in Time.	136
That Included Middle	138
Truth Said	140
On the Cusp of a Poem	142
On a Rubber Duck	143
To My Attention	144
Nietzsche Simplified	145
Earth Prayer	152
Whence The Soul of the Rose	154
The Scandalous Lives of Butterflies	155
A Bowl of Eggs	156
Author's Comments on the Poetic Impulse	159

Thank you to Steve Boint for support and encouragement and for his perspicacious editorial advice and direction.

All Maps Lie

The path dissolves in greenery –
a line followed on paper erased in reality –
and my way forward is lost,
leaving promised destinations undiscovered.

Carefully strewn breadcrumbs now eaten –
the tiny birds momentarily triumphant –
and retreat lost in a maze of random choices,
the vultures gather with larger appetites.
Unmapped paths might lead
to peaks of unexpected joys,
but more roll toward low comedy in dark theaters
where we become jokers on stage,
lost without the benefit of a director.

All maps lie,
but some worse than most –
this one with Borges revenge extracted.
Living in a world of disappearing ink
where disembodied voices lead the uncharted
to coordinates rather than people or places or purposes,
leaves one searching for old vellum maps
with destinations marked with an indelible "X" –
as hopeless a task as searching
for infinitely variable analog tuning
in a stair-step digital world
where technology blurs truth
and there are no new cartographers to trust.

We shall live with lying maps,
painting pictures with large pixels
and nodding with the theatrical simulacrum of life,
forever smiling the mirthless, painted smiles
of the aimlessly wandering clowns we are.

Love in the Wet and Dry

You say my love has evaporated –
your salty tears shed, now crystallized.
How dry say you is my love –
Death Valley dry,
Sahara sere,
oases no longer watered green?

But I proclaim my love is a true flood –
not a desert mirage,
promising, but unfulfilled –
a faithful geyser,
Roman fountains overflowing,
the Seven Seas in expanse,
the mighty Mississippi in strength,
the Angel Falls in height,
our tranquil pond in sincerity.

Perhaps I am crusty and dried out,
a bit wrinkled and unlubricated,
but I will water you
with my own tears of joy,
and you may still bathe in my love.
So, your tears were not in vain,
tears shed to prime my stubborn pump
are not lost even as crystals on your cheek.

Bombus Polaris[1]

Little towns of bumblebees
in the arctic tundra,
alive in the short summer
where time is honey
squeezed in before hibernation.
Cold makes giants in this world –
like little birds flying with aplomb –
but where kings and queens
live happily but one season.
Life at its limits
is its own reason
and its own meter.

---

[1] *Bombus polaris is the arctic bumblebee, one of only two species that live above the arctic circle. Prominent among their adaptations to the demands of the extreme environment is the very large size of the individuals.*

"Supposing Truth…" [1]

No rules of argument needed,
no dogmas of logic,
no Boolean tables or syllogisms,
at their gatherings.
Around the hearth
when fire was still somewhat a novelty,
at the court
with Troubadours' songs echoing,
around kitchen tables
as long as such have existed,
in sewing circles
stitching together order,
they gathered –
with raucous cackling, for sure,
but those conspiratorial whispers,
ripples in a much larger pond –
and truth said.

---

[1] *"Supposing truth were a woman, what then?"* Friedrich Nietzsche, Beyond Good and Evil, *trans. Helen Zimmern, Prometheus Books, Buffalo, NY, Preface, p. 1*

C'est la vie, c'est la guerre, c'est la pomme de terre[1]

Minions of God and country gather
bereft of home, family,
fates uncertain in a foreign place,
hot and dark – like hell imagined –
before that red veil, descending
displaces the horror of imagining
with the living realization.

Tied to maps by strings in the hands of generals,
they are erased on paper and on the field,
without comment by those with swordless hands.
God, wounded one way or the other,
directs them to battle again over the same grounds
with new strings attached.

Much later the few, time-anointed, gather,
strings finally severed and thankfully God forsaken –
old warriors telling their stories,
those unvarnished tales, yet unheard.

---

[1] *"Such is life; such is war; it's a potato"*

Graffiti Reverie

The long train passes slowly and jerkily,
stirring the dust at the California desert crossing,
mostly tank cars and hoppers –
grime-laden, work-worn, boring.
But then the play book openes to box cars –

César lives
in gold on iron oxide red,
with a grape cluster flourish.
And I immediately think of that Milagro beanfield,
irrigation channels, the water community, *campesino* rights,
the merging of cultures beneath the sacred mountain
amidst the southern *Sangre de Cristos*,
all in inimitable Taos turquoise and pink.

el Che rocks
in black on forest green
with a beret.
And Michael in Havana with Hyman Roth,
"I know it was you, Fredo!"
as Fidel, Raúl, and Che kissed Batista good-bye
in Cuba, January 1959,
and I, a high school senior, cheered.

أسامة يفوز[1]
in red on golden yellow
with twin towers aflame.
My internal TV shows
Bush, Cheney, Rumsfeld, and Wolfowitz
on the 88th floor of the South Tower,
just beginning to smell the smoke,
and they did not bring parachutes to work.

Billy Blake swings
in white on black
with a fiery tyger in red relief.
Because I too have visions, inexplicable,
left but to attempt translation
into languages unknown.
Yet to live in abject poverty
with no hands, as ardent angels sing,
drawing images in my brain I cannot paint….

Then the caboose passes and the cross bars lift,
and the car behind me immediately honks.

---

[1] *"Osama wins!"*

Who Are the Pigeons?

They once carried messages, you know,
In little collars nestled in their iridescent neck ruffs.
They told of war,
Infantry thrusts, artillery barrages, cavalry maneuvers,
Or, later, the rolling waves of poison gas.
They told secrets of spies and betrayal,
Warned of ominous weather,
Even carried some mail and had an airmail stamp
Or trailed Genghis Khan over the steppes.

These pigeons know home
Even if it is a cage,
And can find it in darkness or rain
Or if it moves.
That's a talent of their avian brain,
A faithfulness that's unchosen –
Unchosen like the messages they carried,
Messages of despair or elation,
It made no difference.
They are victims of a con game,
But they, least of all, care.

Pigeons are a strange conveyance
Supplanted by less obvious communication –
Less mechanical, less alive.
Those unseen conveyers rely on undulating fields,
Flapping wings in the electromagnetic aether –
Making disturbances to be coded and uncoded –
With a faithfulness that's unchosen.

Pigeons now go about their birdy business
As they always did,
Independent of messages buried in their ruff.
I met one so retired in the park
Pecking popcorn, plump with carbohydrate,
And peacefully innocent of intrigue
Or ulterior purpose,
Rather like a culturally-lobotomized human
Who, however, cannot find his way home.[1]

---

[1] *Pigeons had a new task assigned by humans in March 2016. They have been fitted with "backpacks" carrying sensors for O_3 and NO_2 atmospheric pollutants and fly around London measuring the levels. The mobile sensors give more accurate average values than stationary sensors. After the test with pigeons, some humans will be recruited to carry the sensors, since they tend to wander even more aimlessly than pigeons.*

Panhandle Red Dirt Blues

In the red earth,
beaten adobe hard in harsh light,
taken from others who were lucky to lose,
paths lead to promises only for survivors.

A couple of strands of barbed wire
on twisted blackjack oak posts
stab into the horizon –
a claim made for possession.

A muddy Herford stands
in the stock tank, knee deep,
red muddy water plus shit to drink –
a claim made for sustenance.

The hide-covered, sodded lean-to
blocks some rain and some sun,
and none of the winter wind –
a claim made for home.

Winter wheat in isolated stalks
struggles through cracked red hardpan
under the hot springtime sun –
a claim made for next year.

Much later a solid black road cuts this land
searching for oases of success
past little evidence of struggle –
with red dust covering denied claims.

Untitled[1]
by Steve Boint

Clouds bridge the sliver
of sky between our buildings.
Will you walk with me?

The following was written in response by Lewis:

Late Summer Heat

Clouds bridge the sliver
of sky between our buildings –
billowing, dense, between north and south
with fire at the base upward bound.
I expect to be consigned to fires below,
but not now, not this way,
with kerosene acrid in my throat,
with hot feet, cold prospects.
As heat demons blow our windows –
the hellish grace of choice –
my decision thrusts forward.
I take her hand,
"Come, will you walk with me?"

---

[1]*From private correspondence.*

Headgear to Heaven[1]

Some Jewish males wear *yarmulkes*
and some wear *kippot*,
being careful to trim their hairs
with two-bladed instruments.
The male head covering is
essential for worship,
but Jewish females must not cover
their heads in temple.

Of course, Catholic females
must cover their heads
during the mass,
but only the clergy
wear a *zucchetto* or *pileolus*,
and in a variety of colors
depending on one's station.

Muslim women wear their hair long
and conceal it beneath a hijab.
Men are forbidden to let hair grow long
in a way that would resemble a woman's.
Devout men emulate Mohammed
by growing their beards long
and trimming their moustaches.

---

[1] *The Jewish skullcap is called a* yarmulke (yamaka, *or other spellings*) *from Yiddish or a* kippah *(pl.* kippot) *from Hebrew. The Catholic skullcap is informally called a* zucchetto *or more formally a* pileolus. Kesh *is the Sikh tradition of keeping all hair uncut as a symbol of devotion to "god." The Sikh turban is called a* dastaar. *A cow turd does not require any explanation.*

Buddhist monks shave all hair
to emulate Siddhartha
who removed his hair
as a renouncement of all worldly goods
before his enlightenment.
Many monks also cut off their eyebrows,
although that does not help them see.

Now, Sikh males keep Kesh,
not cutting any of their hairs,
daily grooming their head hair
and winding it under a *dastaar*,
unconcerned by any
Shudra to Brahmin hierarchy.

Diogenes, the cynic, was said
to wear a cow turd on his head
to block the sun
as he reclined in the gutter –
perhaps a shield from the gods as well.

Heaven awaits all so devout,
no doubt.

One Answer to Nietzsche

How shall we comfort ourselves, the murderers of all murderers? What festivals of atonement, what sacred games shall we have to invent? – Friedrich Nietzsche[1]

All those happy people,
where do they all come from?
Just the tip of the advertising stick
prodding your nether regions –
no surprises, advertising is lying
but in a very circumspect way!

Perhaps no more so than unrealistic expectations,
those upbeat messages about life itself,
as terminal and chronic diseases are treated
among legions of smiling, bouncy patients
or as senescence and long-term care are guaranteed
with tender companionship and stimulating activities,
pain and death and isolation left beside the road
as unacknowledged hitchhikers.

Dollars are spent painting the glorious sunshine
of that extended tomorrow
while the debt of dark shadows accumulates,
but that is not a concern of the interests
who discount the future for profit,
nor those on the end of the stick
to whom reality is necessarily foreign
in that space where God once resided.

---

[1] *Nietzsche, Friedrich, The Gay Science, trans. Walter Kaufman, Vintage Books, New York, 1974 (Book 3, ¶125, p. 181)*

Black Shoes on the Move

Calm – moderate the adrenalin rush.
Focus – into some stable moment –
pace … pace … pace ….

The black shoes
like metronomic pistons
flying against the blurred gray,
hypnotic to level the pain against time.
Now, on down the road
the elusive beta-oxidation kicks in
as a momentary relief against the tedium,
the thump-thump slows,
passages clear,
power surges into relaxing muscles
but reaching toward a new plateau of pain.

Back to the black shoes
on the periphery –
the rhythm of the road again:
Step on a crack,
break your mother's back.
Step in a hole,
break her sugar bowl –
step/break … step/break … step/break …
in tune with the black shoes.

Thus, it's only time,
the miles become time,
and the demand winds down
seemingly as all things must
with entropy sufficiently stockpiled,
and the black shoes finally stick to the ground
with lactate glue –
the end so anticipated.

Cave! Cave! Deus Videt [1]

The canvas stretched down the gallery hall,
Long enough to allow a perspective
Unframed and glaringly white-washed,
Palimpsest clean under new oil,
Impasto shadows of my past clinging.
Being there, all seven there:
Hubris haunting creation,
Begrudging the inspiration of genius,
Dissolving under hypothalamic attacks,
Draining to lethargic resignation,
Grasping treasures while able,
And gorging on dopaminergic excess,
Until exhausted in lust satiated –
Plain to see exposed in my white blankness.

My private hell lies in the white heat,
Angel and devil weighing my soul,
Imagining the devil's thumb on the balance.
Just peccadilloes and misdemeanors, no doubt,
Trailing probity circling about the darker center
Beginning to bleed through the white lies –
Blood red, not the new palette searched for.
Cave! Cave!
Too late! Too Late!
Diminishing echoes lost in the neutering whiteness
And the balance tips, the sluice opens
Satisfying the artist whose brush paints still –
The white canvas now awaiting the next reprobate
In the line stretching far through the gallery.

---

[1] *"Beware! Beware! God sees!" is a saying in the centerpiece of* The Seven Deadly Sins and the Four Last Things, *a painting by Hieronymus Bosch, or perhaps a follower of his, completed around 1500. The "seven" are traditionally lust, gluttony, greed, sloth, wrath, envy, and pride. This saying is similar to many biblical warnings, for example: "For God will bring every deed into judgment, including every hidden thing, whether it is good or evil."* Ecclesiastes *12:14.*

Gone

Crossing the lapping margin
between land and sea is always a Rubicon,
even for the girl in the yellow bikini
on the crowded beach on this swimmingly hot afternoon
who cheerily waved nonspecifically as she splashed through.
Is that notice enough to make her part of the family?

Water on a sand-sticky day is always welcome –
in the water as just in life –
and she joined the bobbing population
amidst the sparkles.
Her surreptitious wave from the surface caught my eye once again,
perhaps an intrusion on her sigh,
and she was gone.

BeBop, BeBop

It's right there on that old Blue Note LP,[1]
Monk, Coltrane, Ahmed, and Roy at the Five Spot,
the classic jazz quartet prowling its natural habitat
for sure meaning what they play.
BeBop, BeBop …

Track 1. Crepuscule with Nellie (T. Monk) 3:00
Track 2. Trinkle Tinkle (T. Monk) 10:08
Track 3. In Walked Bud (T. Monk) 11:22
Track 4. I Mean You (T. Monk) 13:53
Track 5. Epistrophy[2] (T. Monk, K. Clarke) 5:19

Piano, tenor sax, bass, and drums
create a nugget of the polyphonic –
sound abstractions like strokes on a canvas
painting chromatic aberrations,
and converting cacophony into flight –

---

[1]The Thelonious Monk Quartet Featuring John Coltrane – Live At The Five Spot Discovery! *Blue Note* – *CDP 0777 7 99786 2 5*

[2]Epistrophy *is a term evidently made up by Thelonious Monk that means the use of repeated sounds at the end of a musical line. (See "epistrophe" as a literary term.) This corresponds to the term "BeBop" which refers not only to the new style of jazz Monk and others helped to create, but to the imitative onomatopoeia of the two-note phrase so often repeated at the end of a 1940s bebop musical line, in which the "bop" is five semitones down from the "be." This is a claim made by Robin Kelley (2009) in* Thelonious Monk: The Life and Times of an American Original, *Simon and Schuster. Other sources suggest that the BeBop term is nonsense language derived from scat singing.*

music alive only in the golden crepuscule of that room,
not heard in full light of the sun.
BeBop, BeBop …

The participatory silence of the jazz cave,
the murmurs, tinkles, gravelly huzzahs,
the trinkle down of bitter spirits,
and that nostalgic hiss in translation –
those are necessary accompaniments.
Through the haze of cigarette smoke
and the growl from the piano,
Bud and Nellie share an epiphany about epistrophy –
BeBop, BeBop …

Behind the Mirror

I dreamed silicon corridors,
silent slabs of unconscious,
tied by unseen compulsive bonds, no doubt,
into patterns of labyrinthine intent.

My vision of random scenes
cut together by that insane film editor
surely tell a story,
were *I* to recall the code.

It's all there packed in closets of time
beyond my ability to open on demand –
some unconscious skill yet hidden –
a blind man with sight, but uncertain vision.

Hard at the center yet is *I*,
wandering after some lollipop sun
crossing behind the celestial haze,
no such star pausing to mark a redemptive birth.

And *I*, the sole inhabitant of this inner cosmopolis,
the puzzler amidst inert atoms,
the chaser of patterns which foresee the future
and claim the past.

I wish for some *Tron*-like partner,
I wish to mesh with the consensual hallucination
of a myriad other *Is*,
down the *Neuromancer* path.

But my weak shadow is my sole companion –
this is my life, my world, always with the same question:
Shall *I* rest in the silent silicon corridor
or continue the quest?

The *David* Forever

The Italian government is to spend €200,000 (£160,000) on a new plinth to support Michelangelo's statue of David after hundreds of earth tremors shook Florence and the surrounding region. – Josephine McKenna[1]

That royal flush in spades
is just one among equals;
likewise,
The *David*, as the perfect fantasy,
is only imagined in flesh.

Yet choice is perverse
and the royal flush always wins
while the fantasy in stone
gets an earthquake-proof pedestal
as real flesh
perishes in the rubble.

---

[1] *http://www.telegraph.co.uk/news/worldnews/europe/italy/11307082/Michelangelos-David-to-get-earthquake-proof-pedestal.html (accessed 05/21/2016)*

Syriana
Syria's piano man sings the stories of the war. – Huffington Post[1]

How could God bring you this scourge?

Amidst fairy tale spires,
playing concerts in the rubble
reveals the human farce –
minarets and church bells calling for peace
to terrorists having no religion.

He lacerates himself – the good refugee,
a trained animal dancing for treats,
smacking that piano in grief and rage –
the beautiful dream lost.

"God stop the world from spinning;
I can't stand it anymore;
I'm dizzy and I want to come down."

There is a little child sleeping in a bed,
hungry, tired but dreaming,
yet the barrel bombs came
not overlooking the small or the old.
The child is up in paradise,
so happy, so full.

Still the out-of-tune piano sounds out the chords
calling the flock to gather.

---

[1] *Charlotte Alfred, "Syria's Piano Man Sings the Stories of the War," The World Post, 3 March 2015. http://www.huffingtonpost.com/2015/03/16/ayham-ahmad-syria-piano-man_n_6848344.html (accessed 10/10/2016)*

The Muffin, Unheated

The crowded diner at midmorning
is that cross-section of demand
where harried servers slide along the transition.
I wanted a blueberry muffin,
unheated, no butter,
to eat with my first cup of coffee.
I thought carefully of the request
as planning is a hard habit to break,
making it as uncomplicated as possible,
but also because that is what I wanted.
The request and the server having passed my attention,
my way was clear for more fruitful contemplation.
Amidst that, my muffin arrived,
steam rising, with a generous side of butter.

The Last Stop Vinyl Shop – NYC, 1995

Bitty was there as usual, culling the new crop
for old funk LPs by George or Sly,
his DJ gig on his mind.
They are all there as you need them –
detritus in a sense
but nostalgia for sale to the right person,
especially one who seeks memories
that either open or close old wounds.

And this day, a worn Artie Shaw 78,
refugee of Grandpa's Victrola combo era,
playing those swing classics and Sousa marches
and broadcasting the afternoon soaps
rife with faux emotion,
but this day opening
near a first recollection of true emotion –
Grandma weeping with the radio
as news of FDR's death poured out.

Those discarded recordings around me –
a searchable catalog of successes and failures,
memories both fictional and real,
both then and now,
can produce real tears.

Coda:
I saw her across the room
head down in jazz, deep in thought,
looking no doubt for that rare Blue Note LP.
And there it was, the reason,
both real and now:
that personal ghost arisen,
perhaps, as I hoped it would.

Ötzi on My Mind[1]

A report that Ötzi the Iceman has 19 genetic relatives living in Austria is the latest in a string of surprising discoveries surrounding the famed ice mummy. Ötzi's 5,300-year-old corpse turned up on the mountain border between Austria and Italy in 1991. – news.nationalgeographic.com (accessed 04/05/2017)

The newest metallurgical technology of 3300 BCE
did not save you – no doubt that copper axe a prized
possession – but older devices, hatred and
the flint-tipped arrow, killed you.

Perhaps you enjoyed your
last meal of red deer and herbal bread and were secure
with leather clothing and soled shoes against the cold,
but those aching joints weighed, not helped by the
shaman's tattoos incised with charcoal, until their pain
was removed at last – after all forty-five years
is a good life for the times.

Sleep well then in that glacial grave.
Dream that even newer technology
will probe your very being, tinged with Neanderthal as it is,
knowing you far better than you knew yourself.
Dream then in satisfaction that those who found
you could have known you, that they share your humanness
and likewise may not be saved by their technology.

---

[1] *Originally published in* Trees in This Neighborhood Remember Me, *Sue Zueger, ed. Scurfpea Publishing, Sioux Falls, 2017.*

The Last Elm

Chestnut memories engrained,
your broad green leaves,
serrated fragile saws they are,
float in the air like oblate lily pads
as samaras boldly pile
in miniature drifts
with vain hopes.
Invisible passenger pigeons roost
and Caroline parakeets call,
those flocks in colored clouds
filmed in black and white
making that fragile record
beyond dusty taxidermy.
But the last elm makes a thousand walking sticks
and a bonfire to dance around,
celebrating something, I'm sure.
The last elm
lives one ring per year
until the last ring
of the last year.

That Old Black Magic

The [nuclear] power plant in question was Northern States Power Company's (NSP) Pathfinder Atomic Power Plant (named after early explorer John C. Fremont, known by Indians as "the path finder") near Sioux Falls, South Dakota – one of two commercial reactor plants designed by the Allis-Chalmers Manufacturing Company. It is also, unfortunately, possibly the least successful commercial power reactor built in the United States. – Will Davis[1]

Pathfinder power
once the dream of limitless energy,
one of those fifties hopes
like paperless offices
and robot servants,
was abandoned in disgust.
The proud atomic symbol on the gate,
the metal sculpture
that proclaimed an artistic revolution,
stands clad in rust
until discarded as scrap.
But life flickers in the sealed core,
a fire that cannot be turned off,
wherever it might be –
another box once opened without regard,
making an artifact
that, once misunderstood,
brings lingering, but certain, death –
another magician
having fooled his audience.

---

[1] *Pathfinder: A Path Not Taken, by Will Davis http://ansnuclearcafe. org/2014/06/13/pathfinder/#sthash.5gUGf3wV.dpbs (accessed 9/11/2016)*

Two Graves[1]

You were the first to plow the land that holds you,
that land so freely given by those who did not own it.
Wheat and corn versus prairie big bluestem –
aliens supplanting old turkey foot win no favors from nature –
yet edible grasses are worth more on the human table,
though they come with that hidden price.

The same sod cut for shelter holds
no grudge as service without sacrifice,
though now the land holds little memory of its past,
conquered as it was by your John Deere steel plow.
Yet it does hold you, like a vice in its steely grip
under such a neatly trimmed lawn and that rocky memorial.

Your well-marked grave is subject to random curiosity
with little thought that the land itself is also a grave,
though lacking granite recognition.
Artificial bouquets on your grave,
as foreign as the crops you planted,
rightly symbolize the repurposing of both you and the land.

---

[1] *Plowing prairie sod, well-anchored by dense plant roots, was slow, hard work and usually required the constant use of paddles to scrape the sticky soil off the moldboard. John Deere, a blacksmith, began an effort to make a more efficient plow. There are conflicting reports, but it appears that Deere's first plows used saw blade steel for the plowshare and smoothly ground wrought iron for the moldboard. Wrought iron could be welded and would reasonably self-scour in heavy prairie sod. Deere's first plow, finished in 1837 at his blacksmith shop in Grand Detour, IL, worked better than any previous plow. In 1838 he built two more plows, one of which was sold to Joseph Brieton, who farmed just south of Grand Detour. That implement was later discovered and purchased by John's son Charles Deere and is on display at the Smithsonian Institution.*

Thoughts to Avoid Late at Night

On the shelf with transistors and lasers
is the "leave-me-alone-box" –
Bell Lab's only "useless machine"
that once turned on
is single-mindedly programmed
only to turn itself off.

Living with innate limits
as products of that rogue, selfish DNA,
we're on the road with Rick Deckard[1] –
using those epigenetic tools
to make up stories that are never true,
trying to become boxes-not-to-be-left-alone.

Aren't we all cast as replicants
desperately in search of purpose
but denied that satisfaction,
only reproducing bodies
that live to be turned off,
if lucky, in three score and ten?

---

[1] *Rick Deckhard (played by Harrison Ford) was the "blade runner" (and perhaps an android replicant himself) in Ridley Scott's 1982 movie,* Blade Runner.

In the Hood

Marinara sauce is not the red of tooth and claw,
but it might fool in dim light of the evening meal –
a thought that popped up somewhat later,
perhaps filtered a bit through a similarly-hued Chianti.
A coil of bloody pasta on the way to my mouth,
its arc was interrupted by the squeal –

one of the most telling leporid vocal responses
and an unmistakable announcement of the bunny's trauma.
Dinner conversation briefly focused on the sonic event,
though no one seemed particularly disturbed,
inured these days as we are to brutal killings of people –
at least this one was quick and efficient.

Between the pasta and the gelato, I rose from the table
for a quick reconnoiter of the execution scene,
still under control of the successful hunter –
who, if undisturbed, based on past behavior,
would devour his supper with gusto,
even returning in darkness to clean up scraps.

I'm not particularly put out to be hosting kitty's feast
on the lawn outside the sunroom windows,
though certain sanitation steps will be required eventually
and another comment must be made to the owner of this marauder –
a gentle woman, but ardent felid apologist,
even as his passerine victims are regularly presented to her.

Only squirrel chattering and scolding, arguably mourning,
from the safety of the overhanging branch
seemed demonstrably troubled –
understandable behavior, having witnessed
that which must be described from his prey perspective
as the brutal murder of a harmless grazer.

I reflected that the squirrel's time will also come,
and likely not a peaceful demise of old age
such as available to the pampered predator.
Hesitantly, and rather soberly, I pictured myself
lovingly being slowly chewed up in some social holding pen
and thought I might hope to meet a much quicker death –
perhaps a bunny's end, sudden and unexpected –
before returning to the more contemporary concerns of my desert.

Well-Behaved Bacon

Well-behaved bacon
Loves the skillet,
Lying in well-ordered strips,
Not rolling up like a pig's tail,
Defying rendering,
And scurrying away
From the spatula.

Of course, those ancestor hogs,
Precursor congenial bacon,
Marched willingly up the runway
Into the slaughterhouse,
Queuing up as if properly British.
And those cooperative pork bellies –
Commodities behaving rationally,
Responding properly to all my options.

Yet, clandestine ghosts,
The salt and fat and nitrites
That will haunt us in the end,
Are just the hidden revenge
Of well-behaved bacon.

The Book of Lascaux

Cave paintings that date to more than 15,000 years ago depict two different kinds of bison, one with long horns and large forequarters ... as well as one with odd-featured shorter horns and small humps. Researchers have long chalked up these differences to artistic imperfection, but new genetic analysis has proven that Ice Age cave artists knew exactly what they were doing. – Nature Communications[1]

Your eye, your thought,
that guided touch that captured seeing –
a delicate detail, that subtle difference
between what is and what is recorded
preserves reality human mind to human mind.

Your modest palate rewards a history
and stretches the story,
enlivening the disappeared hybrids
not as imaginary dreams
or just as relics of their heredity
but as ochre visions and charcoal silhouettes –
inviolate life portraits that give life wisdom.

Those learned pages without writing
instruct those of us
so secure in our imagined knowledge.
We are touched through the millennia
as certainly as if your hand were on our brow.

---

[1]Nature Communications *(2016), DOI: 10.1038/NCOMMS13158*

Falling Down While Sitting in Ecclesiastical Angst
The words of the wise are like goads, their collected sayings like firmly embedded nails – given by one Shepherd. – Ecclesiastes *12:11 (NIV)*

Starlings show an elegance in bulk,
only induced by some neurological abandonment.
To those ends,
murmurations dance in the 10K starling flock –
those unchoreographed phase transitions,
no doubt some epigenetic mass hypnosis –
with the black cloud drunkenly wheeling and dealing,
micromanaged like the smoke rising from an extinguished candle.

And those psychoactive predispositions
inducing some randomly-patterned behavior
lurk like invisible predators in the forest.
My cuddly Marmalade Tigre rolling on the stalk of catnip
is zonked out in a feline reverie,
quite willing to bite the hand that feeds him.
Well that he is not a jaguar hallucinating on yagé vine
 who, logically, would tear out my throat.
At least those Tasmanian wallabies are good for a laugh
frantically hopping in circles in an unproductive escape mode
after sampling the opium poppies.

Or as a special toast to alcohol intoxication –
say hello to Uncle Ted
tying one on at the yuletide wassail bowl,
trashed, though harmlessly under the table.
Not so harmless though –
imagine R. Nixon as the lonely drunk in the situation room
contemplating the red phone.

How many critical decisions have moved our history
made by those buzzed, sloshed, hammered, smashed, or wasted –
like those European starlings three sheets to the wind on fermented berries
choosing looping and crashing for amusement,
sometimes opting to play chicken with a car on the autobahn?
We humans have filled pots of brew as long as pots have been made –
seemingly seeking a taste as vital as sweet or salty.
So, did agriculture get started for the sake of bread or beer?

Is life so hard that every psychoactive substance in the forest
is somewhere on our menu of social forgetting?
Here we are inescapably constrained, the meat of civilization sandwiched
between Apollonian orderliness and Dionysian inebriation.
Partake then: eat, drink, be merry, be wise –
be drunk on them all –
therein lies the God we seek
to escape the agony of the teacher's embedded nails.

By Any Other Name…
Allium sativum (Garlic)

"Rounded bulbs, composed of up to about 15 smaller bulblets known as cloves. Cloves and bulbs are covered by a whitish or pinkish tunic (papery coat). Four to twelve long, sword-shaped leaves attached to an underground stem. Flowers are borne in a dense, spherical cluster on a spike (flower stalk) up to 25 cm long. The young flower head is enclosed in a long-beaked pair of enclosing bracts, which become papery and split to reveal the flowers. Individual flower stalks arise from a common point. Flowers are greenish-white or pinkish with six perianth segments (sepals and petals) about 3 mm long. Bulbils (asexual propagules), which resemble tiny cloves, are often interspersed among the flowers. Flowers usually abort before developing to a stage at which fertilization could take place."[1]

She pealed the garlic clove,
removing the papery skin
and basal membrane
with a paring knife –
a task roughly equivalent
to peeling a grape,
in all its slippery essence.
Nicking the cells starts
an inevitable allicin[2] decomposition
and the release
of volatile sulfides and disulfides
which pass the skin
and flavor the blood,
and are ultimately exhaled
or exuded through skin pores,
rendering one safe
from being eaten by a rabbit.
Now a paring knife is not
the instrument of choice
for mincing garlic.

---

[1] http://www.kew.org/science-conservation/plants-fungi/allium-sativum-garlic, (accessed 06/09/2015)

[2] The principle organosulfur compound present in garlic:

Crushing a clove
with the flat of a French chef,
separates the skin easily,
and then chopping can be done
under the rocking of the blade –
a technique any cook should know.
But technique is personal,
and she preferred sulfide-infused fingers.
Whom am I to question?
I also prefer my grapes with skin intact,
for the record.
Garlic is not a contentious issue
among those on my list,
unless one wants or needs the conflict.
Tread softly and carry a limber cudgel,
tolerate without comment that garlic breath –
might be good advice –
remembering well that *Allium sp.*
is an outlier cousin to the other Liliaceae,
most of whom, after all,
carry a more appealing fragrance.

Watercolor painting by Cathleen Benberg, "Garlic." Used with permission.

Say Hello to David Hume

How much do folks ever really know for sure in this life? How do you know the sun's even going to come up in the mornin'? You don't, that's how! – William W. Johnstone[1]

I'm seeing the leaves come down
once again this autumn –
a predictable marking of the cycle of the seasons.
But, wary of Hume's warning on habituation,
one can never be absolutely certain until the event itself.
I suppose the dinosaurs were shocked
in the way those creatures could have that emotion
when one day the sun did not rise
to shine on their world.
Although my life will probably not
experience such a diurnal disruption –
no doubt the Vegas book would offer you odds –
but that the longer cycle I'm on
doesn't come around in due time,
not even David Hume himself would offer odds.

---

[1] *Johnstone, William W.*, Sidewinders: Deadwood Gulch, *Pinnacle Books*, New York (2011), p. 177

Double Ditch By the River[1]

A place to live –
on the bluff by the big river,
ice-pushed south by the same glacial sheet
that bridged the northern sea for your ancestors.

A place to prosper –
with abundant gardens and wild game,
an excess of sustenance protected against wanderers
by ditches and palisades and the river at your back.

A place to die –
the visible enemies of hunger and pillage conquered,
yet the invisible stalks, uncleansed by the river,
made visible only with your accumulating bodies.

A place to contemplate –
now standing between graves below and contrails above,
past and future sins discussed among the accusing spirits
speaking in the murmurs of the faithful river.
Time frozen in the eye of the artist.
Time rewound in the mind of the poet.

---

[1] *The Double Ditch Indian Village (North Dakota Historical Site) is an abandoned Mandan Indian settlement located on the east bank of the Missouri River about eight miles north of Bismarck, ND. It had a population reaching at least 2000. The settlement was inhabited from about 1500 C.E. to about 1785 C.E. when it was swept by whooping cough, smallpox, and finally by the Sioux. The abandoned village is noted in the journals of the Lewis and Clark expedition on October 22, 1804. The current site is also recorded in the painting, "Missouri River from Double Ditch" (1990, acrylic on canvas), by Sioux Falls, SD, artist Cathleen Benberg.*

LOL

It's mostly fake –
laughter, that is – in the marketplace of mirth,
just another placeholder in discourse, ya' know.
"Funny" isn't necessarily the reason for the jiggling
of neural pathways generating a laugh –
yet pleasure pathway endorphins come with the "real"
but not with the "fake."

"I'm not going to kill you," he said with a chuckle, sheathing his sword
and sending the correct primal signal of safety –
a laugh seriously not funny –
as was the hysterical cackling of those Milgram[1] tools
in horror as the voltages and shrieks climbed.
One might as well have played a sit-com laugh track
as an anonymous simulacrum of mirth.
Something like late night talk show participants
acting out the expected cordiality with merriment,
the same as that which lubricates a dismal cocktail party
with everyone cautious of the potential undercurrent
of dismissive vocal sneering with a generous smile
as a tool of aggression, though short of actual violence.
And someone may always elicit those barrier giggles
shielding one from the atrocious "dirty" joke.

---

[1] *Yale University psychologist Stanley Milgram beginning in 1963 conducted a series of social psychology experiments which measured the willingness of study participants to obey an authority figure who instructed them to perform acts (administering electrical shocks which were actually faked) conflicting with their personal conscience; the experiment found, unexpectedly, that a very high proportion of people were prepared to obey, albeit unwillingly, even if apparently causing serious injury and distress to the subjects. The results were summarized in his 1974 book,* Obedience to Authority: An Experimental View, *published by HarperCollins.*

Or you may have to "laugh off"
your boss' unsolicited sexual advances –
the only predator that should be repelled by not-so-funny laughter.
Sometime try to explain to your kids
why the Three Stooges' violence generates guffaws,
though Larry and Curley aren't smiling.
Beware of "laughing clubs" or that "laughing yoga"[2]
marketing the pretense of an enhanced life experience
equally associated with "real" and "fake" laughing –
just laugh it up because time to reflect can be dangerous.

No doubt genuine mirth is good for you,
activated cholinergic pathways and all,
but the fake is mostly just a crutch of social machinery
allowing cultivation of the necessary talent for being alone
while surrounded by the hell of others.

---

[2] *"Laughter Yoga University" of Dr. Madan Kataria, http://laughteryoga.org/ (12/01/2016)*

Got Lakht[1]

Muhammad, aflame in ascension,
blasphemously illustrated in the *Miraj Nameh*,
while Crusader sculpture
eulogizes Saint Peter animating Tabitha in Nazareth –
where those miraculous pretenders trespass on the promised land –
making art speak for religion, quite apart.

The neat array of limestone blocks of the Western Wall,
looked down upon by the Dome of the Rock,
and nearby in the Old City
the Church of the Sepulcher reposes –
the Abrahamic triad stands boldly,
all praying together, quite apart.

The battlefield is well-trodden ground
with the three-headed monster extant,
in fact more frightening than mythical nine-headed beasts –
though none have learned to kneel,
real or mythical,
and prayers carry swords still, quite apart.

---

[1] *From the Yiddish proverb,* Der mentsh trakht un got lakht. *(Man plans and God laughs.) Also, in translation, the title of a 2015 album by the hip hop group Public Enemy, for the "'hood" point of view. Reasonably, it might also refer to the God revealed in Job, at least until the Hollywood ending. From the Quran:* "Verily, Allah laughs at the despair that His servants feel, even though His Help is so close!" *Somehow, "so close" in the word of a God may be near infinity in the time of men. The Book of Revelation suffices for the laughter of God to the Christians.*

Bludgened by the cross,
scythed by the cresent,
impaled on the spikes of the star,
the blood of martyrs flows so easily –
the message of conquest overwhelms pacific pleas
buried in dusty pages, quite apart.

Forgiveness sheathed,
the blessed and the unblessed,
the same and not the same –
the gods never tire of laughing, all quite apart.

Just Another Poem About Twinkies®

Defying gravity is not a learned skill,[1]
and like a Slinky's® bogus talent
Twinkie® does not have it,
light as it is advertised.
Nor is Twinkie® a sponge,
though it is a cake,
and if wrung the cream is expunged.
For connoisseurs, check out eBay for pre-2013 vintage;
though past the "best-used-by" date,
their water activity is so low
nothing can grow on them
but a little harmless bread mold
adding to their ambiance.
Slinky® is here because it rhymes with Twinkie®,
or *vice versa*,
rather than a figit spinner, Beanie Baby, hula hoop, or pet rock.
And since Slinky® is older than Twinkie®
and "slinky" was even a word before Slinky®.
Old Slinky® toys are also available on eBay –
or so it's said –
though this is a poem about Twinkies®.

---

[1] *http://nerdist.com/why-do-slinkys-defy-gravity/ and "This guy built a floating Twinkie air ship." https://www.gamefaqs.com/boards/164592-fallout-4/73017703*

Life in the Lab Fast Lane, 1963 – 69

Partial Curriculum Vitae Summary: L.C Lewis II
    1963   B.S. in Chemistry
    1967   Ph.D in Physical Inorganic Chemistry
    1967–1969   University of Oklahoma, Research Instructor in Chemistry

The Town Tavern just off campus
was halfway between the lab and home.
Late at night, Sophie would fire the grill
and cook up a cheeseburger or two
if you had not taken a supper break –
and a late night beer was always
a sleep inducer for me.
Breakfast was carb loading for the day
at the Hamburger Inn,
where all I had to do was sit down
and the old Navy guy on the grill
slipped my usual in front of me –
three eggs, a mound of fries, and fried Texas toast,
not forgetting the Louisiana hot ketchup –
all for 99¢.

Not escaping – the lab calls.
What a life –
years in the research lab
with toxic exposures, poor diet,
a basement apartment with a dirt floor bathroom,
but no ulcers,
while John, Malcolm, Martin, and Bobby
were assassinated on the outside
and soldiers died in far places
as someone else's problem.
The work of the lab demanded a confining intensity
and emerging was somewhat like waking –
perhaps you remember the dreams
but the new day comes with shocking reality,
arrows bent and unpracticed skills in demand.

Hopper Here[1]

nighthawks sit here
hawk-nosed

no cigars here
for sale

no future here
or past

no exits here
from it

---
[1] This is an exposition of Edward Hopper's 1942 painting Nighthawks.

Disconsolate Robin

Crouched on the curb,
leeward of a parked car,
shoulders hunched,
down jacket inflated
against the sleet pellets
slanting in from the north,
eying the wormless ground
with faint hopes of breakfast –
pity the disconsolate robin,
that anthropomorphized robin.

Vacation in the Country

Skies that were
Clouds that might
Sunsets where trees
      The winds
Angry limbs

Dusts that mote
Flies that speck
Foxes where hounds
      The chase
Impatient barks

Day to night
Duskward flight
Suns where moons
      The light
Squinting eyes

Skies that are
Clouds that did
Sunsets where tears

1946

The catalpa tree grew beside the back porch of grandpa's house where we lived.
It was the first thing I learned to climb as a kid.
My grandpa told me to stay away from it, but I wanted to climb.
One day I fell out of the tree and landed with a thud and tears.
I remember, he immediately went to get his ax –
He always used to say keep your ax sharp and your gun loaded –
Loosened his double hernia truss,
Which he wore for some reason on the outside of his trousers,
And chopped down the catalpa tree.
He didn't say a word to me.
Grandpa was a man of action.

Black on White

For this Saturday afternoon football,
the black-clad team has the good guys
and the white-clad team the villains.
I'm confused, because I learned
the opposite with hat colors
in B-movie westerns
when I was a kid.
But it's OK –
I've been sensitized by the
 "Black-Lives-Matter" movement,
though tribal connections are difficult to shed.

Celebrating the 4th at Mount Rushmore

Floating in the night sky,
the illuminated monument
evokes the promises and dreams of our nation,
appropriate for this glorious celebration
of "life, liberty, and the pursuit of happiness!"

Yet viewed close-up through a telescope,
its surface conveys a less pristine message –
rather like moving from the forgiving light
and soft textures of an intimate restaurant,
into the harsh fluorescent reality of the restroom.

Of course both perspectives are valid,
and most people choose one or the other, not both,
and perhaps some are still supporters of the King.

Azalea Days[1]

day dreams floating through the dreams
sea foam in a green sea night
curious coincidences compound
during those
azalea days, magnolia nights

if it were only a dream
one might think it fiction
but there was no awakening
and the fiction realized
drowning in green sea stories

life asail on a following sea
floral fragrances abound
measuring the limits of dreams
as the sleep of night
transforms the aroma of day

---

[1] *Azaleas have odorless blossoms, an uncommon property among the familiar southern blooming plants. Is it necessary that they somehow compensate for their insufficiency?*

Alto Bitter Blues[1]

my sax-o-phone
a-moan

in a dark song
all wrong

bitter whiskey
kiss me

you sax-o-moan
a-lone

---

[1] *Originally published in* Trees in This Neighborhood Remember Me, *Sue Zueger, ed. Scurfpea Publishing, Sioux Falls, 2017.*

Notes on the Return of LSD in 2017
"You're not Tripping: LSD is Making a Comeback."[1]

Postage stamps no longer need to be loaded and licked, which is a good thing to avoid – for a variety of reasons – like most activities in the back seat of Ken's bus.

Analytical grade, ashless filter paper was always a better choice if available – sanitary and digestably harmless, as well as reasonably variable in the load it can absorb.

There is no quick test I'm aware of which establishes the purity and potency of a product – it's best to just know your neighborhood, as always.

Many have asked me about potentially harmful "acidic" properties, given its German name, lyserg-säure-diäthylamid (LSD) or lysergic acid diethylamide in English, and the fact that it's called "acid."

But it's not an acid, rather the amide of the acid, and amides are neutral, neither acidic nor basic to any appreciable extent – another explanatory triumph of Pauling's theory of resonance, not that this fact makes much of an impression on most folks.

I cannot tell you what to do if the sky unzips; it mostly depends on what emerges for you out of the rip, and I am by no means a Freudian practitioner – ask Lewis Black, not Cliff Lewis.

That said, good luck on your adventure. Don't call me!

---

[1] Diana Kruzman, *"You're not Tripping: LSD is Making a Comeback,"* Sioux Falls Argus Leader, *30 July 2017, p. 8B*

I Repeat

At a singular age with loss,
I awakened with pain,
and pain and pain and pain,
and pain and pain and pain,
and pain and pain and pain,
and pain and pain and pain,
and pain and pain and pain,
and pain and pain and pain,
and pain and pain and pain,
and pain and pain and pain,
and pain and pain and pain,
….
Like prayer beads fingered,
counting breaths in meditation,
meaning departs in noise –
a strange trance.

On Cranes (Not the Birds)

I wonder what the Egyptians would have built
given a construction crane –
perhaps something more monumental,
combining hubris with a newer tool?

No doubt that would have spared slaves,
though now cranes lifting
precast brick and mortar walls
spare masons from employ, as well.

And a new construction devise
can become a new destruction device –
swinging that wrecking ball
effortlessly wrecking history.

Yet there is a skyhook quality
in those cranes lifting steel girders to the 99th floor
to fuel those Mohawk ironworkers
keeping a riveting tradition alive.

It's all a matter of give and take
what you can do with levers and pulleys,
natural tools so industriously
put to unnatural uses.

Mud on My Face

I regret not detouring when that sign appeared,
but muddy roads are a strange attractor
and mud-wrestling babes are down the road –
it's the Uncle Meriwether, Big Muddy gene
that makes muddy soup a food group for me.
I proved that if you get more than waist deep in Big Muddy,
be prepared to sing those Muddy Waters' blues.
But you've got to follow Big Muddy into the mountains
to find that peaceful ocean on the other side
or mud's your name with higher-ups,
not that you can avoid mud-slinging with the natives
or stepping on the stray mud cat along the way
or being reduced to eating mud hens.
Though I never got beyond the muddy road
and ended up in that muddy bog
of forever being a stick-in-the-mud,
and those mud-wrestling babes
just turned out to be cows.

Love, Incidentally[1]

I.
You blew in on a blue northerner
and left tamed, or someone was tamed.
What do you call it
when it's less than a one-night stand?

II.
You were all in for passion,
you were all in for me.
I outlasted your passion –
the bargaining begins.

III.
Walking hand-in-hand
makes for a different journey.
I wish you hadn't
gone your own way.

---

[1]*Originally published in a slightly different form in* Trees in This Neighborhood Remember Me, *Sue Zueger, ed. Scurfpea Publishing, Sioux Falls, 2017.*

IV.
A toasted baguette spread with saffron aioli
dipped into bouillabaisse[2]
brings the meadows and seas out of memory,
but always a danger in approximating the real –
so easy with love.

V.
Love has those personal passions, of course,
and touch sets the senses on fire,
but you're really not "in love"
until you are documented on Instagram.

---

[2]*See James Patterson's recipe for bouillabaisse with aioli, https://www.brownetrading.com/recipe/petersons-bouillabaisse/ and an aside from a novel, by Louise Penny, https://books.google.com/books?isbn=1250022126, p. 37 (accessed 02/16/2017).*

Five Women: Mostly True Love Stories

He was somehow incomplete,
But an inner gentleness compensated
So that relationships were possible.
He once told me, late in life,
No relationship *he* initiated ever lasted –
But five women chose him and loved him.

Linda, the bespectacled Jewish law student
    Who was his former student
    And decided he was the only one for her!
    Her father said it was OK,
    Since he was already circumcised.

Stephanie, the sophisticated, elegant dark beauty,
    Whose cool appearance
    Created a bubble around them at parties,
    And whose straightforward, "I want you,"
    Was the correct thing to say.

Roberta, Bobbi, the earthy party girl,
    Who pulled him away from the wall,
    Made him ride the roller coaster,
    And blew away his pessimism.
    "Let's start with sex and see what happens!"

Danielle, the wife of a colleague,
    Whose unhappiness was swept away
    When she opened up with him.
    They began her new life,
    And she took charge to complete it.

Mary Ann, the "older" woman,
    Intellectually and emotionally more mature than he,
    Who fed him and led him,
    More like a sister than a lover,
    Fulfilled, but with an easily-ignored tinge of incest.

He married one of these five women,
A long-lasting and pleasurable relationship,
Recently ended with his death.
He loved his wife and she knew it.
He also told me that he loved them all,
That it was a comfort to him
To construct all the possibilities,
Accompanied by no regrets whatsoever.
Diversity, after all, can be a virtue!

McSonnet

Quarter Pounder with cheese, proudly displayed
in color graphics on the menu board,
no doubt an epicurean treat
with just six miles of calories to burn.

Be advised you're not eating its picture –
the model is never reality!
Quarter Pounder is a stage character,
make-up applied to be seen from the seats.

The theater corner tiles are slippery
with a thin film of overheated oil,
fitting partner to the limp lettuce leaf,
pallid pickles, and tasteless tomato.

Free Wi-Fi with its built-in hacking calls
to engage your attention while you "dine."

Something Says Nothing

The ghost of minimalism
leaves invisible footprints.
My words mouth meaninglessness
with white font on white paper
neutralizing the only content line:

. . . .

And given a monotonic Theremin
serenading the titanium oxide white canvas[1]
displayed in the unlighted gallery,
accompanied by a blind, deaf pianist
pounding the keyboard of a hammerless piano,
how much less do you want from a poem?

Try,

XANAX + SELECT 🖱 + DEL

Nothing Says Something.

---

[1] *For example, see works by American minimalist painter Robert Ryman, which have sold for up to $15 million.*

The Undistorted Communication Game, *Sans* Jürgen Habermas

Rule of the Game: Draw a line from the particular trope on the left to its bulleted definition on the right.

That ideal speech situation,
so long sought through
"undistorted communication"
is cleverly just plain talk, absent lies.
But, take away pedantic Habermas
and add trope (e.g.

metaphor
simile
analogy
synecdoche
metonymy
simulacrum)

to make it
rhetorically interesting.

Herr Professor Doktor Habermas
overlooks the possibility
that ennui becomes the main enemy
of undistorted communication.

---

trope: a word, phrase, expression, or image used in a figurative way, e.g.

- *the word for part of something used to mean the whole (boots for soldiers)*

- *one thing used or considered to represent another (life is a circus)*

- *an artificial representation or image of something (statue of God)*

- *comparison between different things that are similar in some way*

- *comparison between two different things, usually using "like" or "as" (like a rolling stone)*

- *an attribute of something used to stand for the thing itself (Washington for U.S. government)*

Going to School

Sadie, the black lab prison guard –
without opposable thumbs
and with pink tongue lolling –
learned to sniff-out clandestine cell phones
facilitated by someone nasally deprived.

Concurrently she induced her teacher
to supply, with clockwork regularity:
room and board,
medical care,
companionship,
and, most importantly, a repeatedly-thrown Frisbee.

The hierarchy here is uncertain.

Over and Out

voices to shepherds
about angels and virgins
and times coming
left and right brains
bicameral conversing
tell you a secret
I hear those voices
apocalyptic
suggestions prompts
anticipating solutions
my radio with no knobs
off/on volume tuning
someday I may follow
those exhortations

Love Lessons Learned

Love lessons learned
take a while to sink in,
and perhaps time is necessary
to get a lesson repeated.

She had eyes Rembrandt
might have painted
and an affect drawn straight
from Munch's Norwegian humor.

Sometimes I saw her as blue
Picasso might
or through the sepia wash
of Gauguin,

but I never saw her revealed
with my glasses on.
Suffering from love of love
makes illusions real.

Books

The old kind with boards and paper –
on my shelf in neat arrays,
lasting a thousand years if you want,
subject to Fahrenheit 451,
sort of portable, depending on how many you want to carry.

The digital kind with 0s and 1s –
in my pocket, just a small bulge,
invisible content instantly transmittable,
depending on viable technology to access,
ephemeral and immaterial in the wrong kind of energy field.

Media is a distraction, not the message!
Sophocles is alive in either.

Galileo at the Mill[1]

Blind in his last days
under bondage and exile
by the Catholic Philistines of the Inquisition,
he jousted with nature as ever,
his mill of science turning,
grinding the threat of torture to dust.

Now fallen from the heights of power
where his heresies were the chains
that pulled down the columns
of the temple of Ptolemy,
he is eyeless in Florence,
slave only to the demands of natural law.

This impossible Beethoven of Physics
diluted gravity to remove its shroud,
teasing out its secret number
by endlessly rolling those polished brass balls
down the slanted boards –
from rolling balls to turning planets.

In revenge for seeing the instruments of torture,
he sent word of his two new sciences
out of Italy to the Protestant North,
washing away the pillars of Mediterranean science
by transferring his power to the newborn Newton
destined to become the Pope of Physics.

---

[1]*Reference is to a line from Milton's "Samson Agonistes": "Eyeless in Gaza at the mill with slaves, himself in bonds under Philistian yoke…" At age 30, Milton visited Galileo, blind and under house arrest, in Florence. Milton's great work (e.g. his own cosmological epic,* Paradise Lost*) was ahead of him. Perhaps this visit also impacted Milton, encouraging his participation in the English civil wars beginning in 1642 as polemist for the Commonwealth in defense of state freedom.*

Hopes Considered

Read of imagined pain and woe hanging
    among writers who do not know
        real human pain and suffering,
            or glorified evils as an easy poetic target
                for those who can only imagine
                      what the depth of real evil could be.

                Perhaps we need another Great War,
        a forest fire for civilization
      to cleanse the writing palate
    where the view from the ruins
  makes celebration a goal once more,
pain and evil disappearing in the mundane.

Some hold that War gives meaning to existence,
    exposing woes of realized pain and unrepentant evil –
        thinking poetry survives War
            as Great War takes down technology –
                where poetry then becomes a necessary song,
                    as a longed-for purposeful grace.

                Yet what madness could hope for War –
      a solution from that vengeful God-of-Noah?
    From whom does such a God seek absolution?
    Poetry can never gain from such a sin,
  souls lost compound to souls lost and to souls lost, …
and poets cannot cry loudly enough to reconcile that.

The Cherry Tree

I must tell you of my old cherry tree,
amidst the litter of discarded twigs and bark shed
with twin trunks near split
and that scar of a large limb lost to ice
but saved as wood carved, not to burn.

Now, naked branches scratch at clouds,
waiting patiently, as a tree does, to cherry again –
given its age, uncertain of its next spring –
pining as a cherry tree might for its old Michigan home
closer to the forest than the prairie.

Perhaps in its own way
a tree waits to welcome the robin cherry pickers
who distribute its seeds
in purple-hued watercolor paintings
over the nearby grounds and walks.

My uncomplaining companion,
having watched three generations of family
pass by under its sheltering limbs,
never wonders of its existence or fate
except through me.

Should there be a broader consciousness
through which we the living may communicate,
then I shall imagine that I would be proud
to share and perpetuate your memories,
cherry-imbrued as they may be.

One Day Soon

She's taking another of those hot-water-depleting showers
wasting all that purified fluid and precious energy.
This morning I found the milk carton in the fridge door
where it's not cold enough
and the butter dish on an inside shelf
where butter gets too cold to be spreadable –
hey, that's the reason for the butter keeper in the door.
What's so difficult about having objectives?
That list I'm silently carrying around in my head
has several more items for discussion.

No doubt she will be leaving soon –
all the tendencies are there.
I really had hopes for this relationship
and was willing to bend my necessities almost to breaking.
As usual, I won't know until after she leaves
whether I will feel regret or relief.

Dimethylcadmium[1]

Superlatives are compelling
as logical solidarity amidst chaos –
thus so, for toxicity.
Biding time gracefully,
it resides in my freezer,
a snugly ampuled, cradled liquid
modestly straw yellow
and visually innocuous –
hiding that breath of death
where danger speaks to banality

---

[1] *Dimethylcadmium (H_3C-Cd-CH_3) is the most toxic substance known on a molecule-per-molecule basis.*

Starstruck

They're a bit like indoor stars,
just as bright, but unnoticed by day.
They are all about nightshine
through the shadowed rooms
prowled by one sleepless,
awakened to restless anticipation.

Those silent sentinels or watchers stand,
sometimes disconcertingly,
against something or for something –
in red, green, blue, amber, yellow, white.
I count exactly thirty-one stars
in my personal celestial sphere.

Just another technological intrusion,
reminders of tasks or duties or devices.
But I will admit, they can also be comforting
like receiving a new email or text,
feeling acknowledgement
no matter how remote or dispassionate.

Once rendered starless by a storm,
I sought comfort in the few with battery backup.
I shall probably deny it in good measure,
but I have symptoms of being starstruck,
which does not help with insomnia
though stars do aid navigation in a pitch black room.

My Thirty-one Stars:

tablet:	green (1)	desk lamp:	red (10)
DTA box:	green (2)	cable box:	green/blue (11,12,13)
printer #1:	blue/white (3,4)	modem:	blue/yellow (14,15,16,17)
printer #2:	amber (5)	laptop:	white/red (18,19,20,21)
router:	green (6)	telephones:	green/red (22,23,24,25)
shredder:	green (7)	power strip:	red/green (26,27)
speaker #1:	green (8)	USB extension:	blue (28,29)
speaker #2:	red (9)	smoke detectors:	red (30,31)

Negotiating Desire

Many years ago –

I turned from her once again
tinged with fear of rejection
and fear of acceptance –
friendship, but more, the gamble.

Desire is a wanting seed
whose growth is uncertain when shared.
Yet reaching out would seem so natural,
embracing so satisfying.

I feel the bond,
the easy possession of unspoken love
only the nature of which in doubt
in a tangled net of relationships.

So we drift here, together and apart
tortured by vagaries of attraction and repulsion,
both guiltily unfulfilled in some sense,
unwilling to gamble so much on desire –

after these many years.

Copernicus at Rest

Copernicus on his death bed
clutching the book[1]
reflects the still of the night.
When he lies silent and unmoving
with drapes closed and heavy hanging,
he dreams of the other world –
the one he created
where even the dead move.
The Holy Father blesses him,
uncomprehending of his portent,
so certain that the center of the Church
was the unmoving center of it all.
Copernicus' sigh welcomes death,
leaving the Earth alive with his message.

---

[1]*De revolutionibus orbium coelestium (On the Revolutions of the Celestial Spheres), espousing the heliocentric theory of the solar system, was published in 1534, just before Copernicus' death.*

The Waiting Room

Waiting in common,
though uncommonly gathered
and arrayed randomly,
this strange family
of strangers congregates,
each the same and each special.

There is a clock,
though it times inconsistently
without interest in time itself,
as if scheduling events uncertain
with no ballads or epic tales foreseen
or patience recognized.

The door opens
and one less or one more waiting
as waiting weights are reweighed
for those still waiting
with that common goal
in the waiting room.

"From My Cup of Tea"[1]

Macarons, confetti cookies –
rather grossly stated –
live best in Paris,
probably on the *Place de la Madeleine*,
filled with Belgian chocolatier's crème
or perhaps yuzu, matcha, and black sesame seeds.
Yet Proust demurs –
respectful of his history as another person –
for dipping preferring the classic madeleine
void those primary party colors
or matcha green tea flavors,
though the plain ambience is quite expensive –
it's not as if anything else is worth remembering.

---

[1]*Marcel Proust.* Remembrance of Things Past, *Trans. C. K. Scott Moncrief, Random House, New York, 1934, p. 36*

Academic Vaudeville

Old academic acts are comfortably stale and cheap,
and their window to the world is tiny and grimy.
Listening to them is similar to mining
I Love Lucy, My Little Margie, and *Father Knows Best,*
for advice on dealing with family relationships.

The Play Bill:
Sigmund, Karl, and Jean-Paul appearing nightly,
neither alive nor relevant, but compelling,
explaining the logic of war as a necessary human behavior.
There will be name calling,
and perhaps academic blood will be shed.

Sassy Sigmund, crazy Karl, and jimmied Jean-Paul
twirl in *pas de trois*:
dialectical ids jousting with existential angst,
surplus value squeezed by bucolic bureaucracies,
superego supremacy challenged by bad faith.

Structured chaos and rampant perspectivalism
will prevail as they debate who is alive and who is dead –
not including God, who is covered by another act.
As Jew, Jew/Lutheran, and Catholic,
they find justifying anything rather easy.

Opening for the trenchant trio will be
the bearded lady, monkey boy, and a two headed calf –
J-P will provide accordion music as an encore
while S&K share cigars with the audience.
"This way to the EGRESS!"[1] – A Bonus Act!

---

[1] *When P. T. Barnum found that customers stayed too long when visiting his American Museum in New York City, he posted signs pointing to a door saying, "This way to the egress." When people went through the door expecting another exhibit, they were outside and the door locked behind them, forcing them to buy another admission if they wanted to see more.*

A Crow Bar "True" Story in First Person

Sophie, from behind the bar, had a delousing plan.
She asked me to pretend to be her uncle
and tell the little loser who always sat on the last stool
to cut it out with his flirting and suggestive comments to her.

I was a regular in front of Sophie, and for sure not her uncle,
but had from time to time helped her son,
who was also a regular in the corner booth after school,
with his algebra homework.

But why she asked me this favor was not obvious
beyond the fact I was a wiry and tough old gray-beard
who perhaps seemed harmlessly attentive to her and her son.
The bar rat was obnoxious, no doubt,

and I was tired of his loudmouth behavior as well;
yet I was also a bit chagrined about
how she had apparently categorized me,
asking for a favor because there would be no strings attached.

Am I really that harmless, after all,
with no possible other sort of attraction to her –
meaning that sort of thing is all over for me?
Reality is sometimes slow to sink in

and usually carries a painful shock when it does.
Now some months later, I still have not answered the question
or even bothered to carry out any research –
Sophie must be a good bartender with spot-on evaluations.

By the way, the rat was exterminated,
the boy and I have moved on to geometry,
and Sophie remains bartenderly attentive
with an offer of a free beer for my tutoring.

Horn Island[1] Blues

See a wilderness declared by human hand
and nature's proclivity,
where the great blue herons stomp their feet
and the gulls annoy only other gulls.
See plastic detritus reposited on white beaches
declared by nature's meandering, Gulf gyre,
and human proclivity.
A sandy skeleton slightly rising in sight of shore,
its highest white dunes surfacing like the great white whale,
is a destination unsought even by hermits.
Some alluvial relic, in the way of hurricanes
and lone survivor of the battles of Boreas and Notus,
waits patiently for the churning seas
to silently submerge its gentle peak –
nature's hand on its brow not so tenderly,
in a measured response to the compulsion of human excesses.
Abandoned by those who used it because it was abandoned,
leaving only the earth-bound raccoons
for whom there will, alas, be no ark for escape in the end.

---

[1] *Horn Island is a barrier island in the Gulf of Mexico, eight miles offshore from Pascogoula, MS, about ten miles long and 3000 feet wide, rising to a maximum height of 20 feet above sea level.*

Toxic Principles

Partially written in the style of Gerard's Herbal.[1]
Ranunculus acris (Tall Buttercup)

"Stems slender, erect, up to 1 meter tall. Principal leaves palmately divided into 3 – 5 segments, long-petioled, the blades cordate in outline. Flowers solitary at the ends of terminal or axillary pedicels, the yellow petals 10 – 12 mm long. Occasional along roadsides or in abandoned yards. Escaped or persistent after cultivation. May – July." – Theodore Van Bruggen[1]

Johannus Whittle writeth:
Ranunculus, Crow-foot, Butter-floures –
Diverse sorts of permitious herbes,
Layeth a toxic principle of most violent force.
These herbes require exquisite moderation,
Not to be taken alone.
With due maner of temperance,
Mixed with benign spirite are profitable,
And draweth forth flegmaticke humors from the chests.

Benedictus writeth:
Yellou butter-cup provideth against the pain of tooth.
Folke tie this herbe stamped with salt unto a finger,
Thereupon causeth greater paine in the finger
Than holds in the tooth,
By meanes whereupon the greater paine disposes of the lesser.
Vagabond beggars do stamp leaves,
And apply to cheekes or arms,
Causeth pustulous ulcers we see daylie displaed,
That these cunning ply more to move the people to pittie.

---

[1]Leaves from Getrard's Herball, *ed, Marcus Woodward, Dover Books, New York, 1969.* All of the archaic spellings are taken from the book and the sentence structure tries to mimic that found in the book.
[2]Van Bruggen, Theodore. The Vascular Plants of South Dakota, *Iowa State University Press, Ames, 1976, page 226*

This versifier writeth:
Ranunculus acris flew into this continent with the Europeans,
Bringing its toxic acid principle,
Still so useful to those cunning beggars in third world bazaars –
My pernicious little frog – cultivar rampant!
Those European forefathers, my ancestors,
Seeking that golden treatment in escape,
Deposited likewise on this continent other toxic principles –
Toxic first to others,
But ultimately self-reflexively toxic:

An invocation of manifest destiny –
That they were the ones chosen to inherit this vast continent,
To the exclusion of those aboriginal occupants.
No Golden Rule here!

The germ of the idea –
That enslaving other, "inferior" humans was desirable social behavior,
So rational by economic metrics.
No Golden Rule here!

A kind of misogyny –
That women are defined relative to men, rib derivatives,
Secondarily significant to male purpose.
No Golden Rule here!

Whig analysis aside, the wrongs yet weigh heavily –
Yellow, acidic corrosiveness that cries to be fully neutralized.

In the Country, I Note

crack and rumble
of the rainstorm
comes out and down
and comes up as corn
in tall green rows
and turns into herds
drinking from muddy ponds
and turned soil furrows
following the plow
by the graveled roads
leading to wind-rowed
white-boarded houses
and timber-framed barns
with slanted roofs
that deflect the downpours
filling the ponds
watering the rows
muddying the roads
flushing one life
uncuriously noted
by those innocent of the rain

Innovation

the point is to
disrupt

a honed-iron edge
forged

a furrow must
follow

gulls soar in its
brown wake

Laissez Faire

join me here
in free fall
an assignation with words
that lover's leap
in braless exuberance
with license to scribble
dangerous like unprotected sex
with those wordless expressions
giving meaning without words
those expressionless words
written to obscure meaning
defining syntax as you compose
with reckless abandon
to do or not do
is no-net writing
it's all out of bounds
because there are none
all games are scoreless
and no such thing as par
no rule except there is no rule
laws of friction temporarily suspended
big G and little g both zero
floating naked words
or cloaked words
who, whom, I, me in limbo
where even neatness doesn't count
and editors are extinct
let go and join me here

Bus Token Taken Without Response

I gave a bus token to a guy panhandling at the bus stop;
he accepted it without response.

They're mostly students, laden with book packs,
departing campus in early darkness for whatever passes for home.

The light above my seat flashes on and off,
as the bus bounces along, heading south past the stadium.

Stopping frequently, anonymous individuals exit,
wordlessly disappearing into the lowering mist.

The regular driver, resigned to his thankless task,
and in a moment of recognition, says, "Tomorrow," as I exit.

The bus is gone, the riders have slipped transparently into the night;
I am here today, in the dark about "Tomorrow."

At the Faculty Club

2015
I survey the room –
quiet conversation,
a point delivered with obvious satisfaction,
appreciative laughter at the erudite joke,
ominous anticipations of hypothetical events,
careful analysis of contingencies,
an academic murmur –
I withdraw silently,
having been there too frequently.

2016
The background is white noise,
through which the volcano eruption cuts –
Aureolus Philippus Theophrastus Bombastus von Hohenhein,
reincarnated –
a new standard for conversation,
like Maria Callas singing in the church choir.
Even though the room was sparsely populated,
I withdraw silently,
since there was no room left in the room.

The Answer to the Old Riddle That Cannot Be Asked in Writing

Looking around at the early-morning coffee shop patrons,
I'm the only one shuffling paper.
Several people have smart phones out –
listening, speaking, texting, flipping through screens.

A couple of tablets I see are online –
the one at the next table playing the CNBC live telecast.
No one seems to be paying attention to the TV
over the counter, inaudibly tuned to CNN.

Not meaning to conflate "habit" with "correctness,"
I prefer to read the physical newspaper – no longer so read all over.
I'm told by some, though,
it makes an annoying, rustling sound as the pages are turned.

Poet's Day Off

today I'm at peace with this cruel world
just coasting along
maybe a day off
naturally the world goes on
large and small
rabbits grazing on tulips
squirrels stealing from birds
all within but beyond my notice
I don't ache when news comes on
not moved by the latest atrocity
or the morning bloviation
because I'm tuned out
unpunctuated
lassitude bound
proudly apathetic
soaking in the tub
bathing in insouciance
worshipping at the temple of indifference
it's my day off
so I'll write about that

Scientists At the Wall

I. Chemist's Dilemma
No solace
in understanding
the toxin
that kills you.

II. Fritz Haber[1]
Understanding how to make a poison gas
is quite different from making a poison gas.
It went around and came around.

III. Improvident Physicists for Hire
A sweet problem, after all,
and if we don't,
someone else will.

---

[1] *Haber was a German chemist, a Jew, a Nobel Prize winner, and a German national hero after his work on chemical weapons in WWI. He went into exile in 1933.*

Optimistic Pessimist

world worn
vitality drained
few
dragged down by
many
moist clouds
desiccated
fertile fields
forced fallow
hope
a glimmer
pink sunrise
sharp mind
fresh thought
same end
night falls
again
not unexpectedly

Gimme Shelter[1]

At that time when there were no memories before,
I remember her gathering arms.
I remember her little house behind ours
Filled with flowers from the trash pile of the cemetery.
The cornbread and milk lunches,
Sprinkled with sugar sometimes as a special treat,
Her wash tubs and hot irons – don't touch!
That she called me "Little Mister,"
That she was suddenly gone.
But mostly,
I remember her gathering arms.

---

[1] *Originally published in* The Scandalous Lives of Butterflies, *ed. Kevin L. Cole, Scurfpea Publishing, Sioux Falls, 2015.*

Photoautotrophs

They drink the sun,
And exhale the air,
With no comprehension.

We huddle
Before the hearth
At their pleasure.

As those so relegated,
We ask:
Is it better
To understand
Your limitations
Or be ignorant
Of your superiority?

Cycle Interrupted, 1948

A creek ran behind the local cemetery.
Along its bank funeral leftovers were discarded –
Mostly graveside florals,
Losing their bloom about as rapidly
As memories of the recently-interred fade.
From time to time,
The cemetery caretaker burned the rubbish pile,
Reuniting the flowers with the soil
And the air from whence they came.
Once, happening upon this unintended ritual,
It occurred to me,
This was a more desirable fate
Than that experienced by the cemetery occupants,
Trapped as they are,
Toxified inside their underground vaults and coffins –
Not that it makes any difference to them,
Or most of the people who put them there.

The Tuned Eye

*Gentiana andrewsii (*Bottle Gentian*)*
Corolla bottle shaped and almost closed at the top when in flower. Stems 3 – 6 dm
tall, single or few from a perennial base. Leaves ovate-lanceolate, up to 10 cm long.
Inflorescence a dense, sessile cluster of flowers terminal or in the upper 1 or 2 leaf axils.
Extremely rare in wet meadows over the state. Aug. – Sept. – Theodore Van Bruggen[1]

A stroll through the prairie can be whimsical and purposeful.

This day I sought the bottle gentian,
among the native grasses and forbs,
as a good excuse –
like the medieval knights
on sight-seeing trips through Europe and the Holy Lands
in the guise of a holy quest –
to spend time on that land-locked sea,
riding with the waves which carried me,
out of sight and out of mind.

In a slight depression, green and moist,
I became aware of it at my feet,
sharing space with a tuft of blue grama
and an immature Missouri goldenrod.

How easy to be simultaneously elated and deflated.

That place is not holy ground,
but is personally sanctified to the extent
that I can still recognize the very spot.

---

[1]*Van Bruggen, Theodore.* The Vascular Plants of South Dakota, *Iowa State University Press, Ames, 1976, page 348.*

Duly documented,
no doubt in the tradition of Professor Andrews,
and therefore rendered mundane,
I left the bottle gentian undisturbed
to continue its solitary cycle.

But not so solitary!

Now there were others —
a family, a tribe, a city of gentians,
circling and marching around me
no matter which way I turned.

Now I'm not so sure about Professor Van Bruggen,
as my treks to marshy prairie meadows
are rare when I do not meet a bottle gentian —
they flick into existence at the least provocation —
his "extremely rare"
did not specify a "p" value of significance.

Rarity is in the eye,
since, of course, you cannot see many until you see one.

I wonder what else I shall see on this prairie,
that is already there,
but invisible to my untuned eye?

A Sunny Afternoon in April ....

God is dead. God remains dead. And we have killed him. – Friedrich Nietzsche (1887)[1]
The fate of our times is characterized by rationalization and
intellectualization and, above all, by the disenchantment of the world – Max Weber (1917)[2]

The Pueblos, undisturbed, were not hostile,
But the terrain was harsh and particularly unforgiving
For those *campesinos* on the frontier.
And it was, after all, a wilderness,
From their perspective,
So their abandonment by the Church was just another challenge.[3]

How then are those enchanted, abandoned souls to behave in ritual?
How to mark the cycle of the seasons,
    The cycle of the ceremony,
    The cycle of life and death?
How to tolerate the randomness of existence unexplained –
    But accept and expect and worship,
Imagining His very blood dripping from the illuminated crags above them.

The symbolic cross became their material cross,
Hewn, erected, and utilized.
The imagined wounds became real and recorded dutifully as scars,
    Pressing cactus spines into His forehead,
    Stripping bare of flesh His back with yucca branches.
His journey of the cross became the daily journey of those enchanted in the wilderness.

---

[1] Nietzsche, Friedrich, The Gay Science, trans. Walter Kaufman, Vintage Books, New York, 1974 (Book 3, ¶125)
[2] Weber, Max (1946). "Science as Vocation", in From Max Weber, tr. and ed. by H. H. Gerth, and C. Wright Mills. New York: Free press. (Originally given as a lecture in 1917.)
[3] Mexico became independent of Spain in 1821, at which point the Spanish withdrew their Benedictine and Jesuit missions. The Hispanic communities, especially on the frontiers, were bereft of church support.

So, strolling leisurely on a bright April, Easter afternoon,
Remarkably at ease and unchallenged,
I passed the mansions of Christ,
Boxes to box enchantment,
Filled with Nietzschean echos,
Stately and well-adorned by appropriate symbols,
With ample free parking,
But empty and lonely this sunny, Easter afternoon.

Seeing the church, symbolic of abandonment by disenchanted congregations,
I thought of the *Hispanos Penitentes* of long ago,
Church-abandoned in the shadow of the *Sangre de Cristos*,
Along what would later become the high road to Taos.

Those disenchanted here and now have not abandoned ritual,
But the center of that life has shifted
And is surrounded with new rituals unrecognizable in the enchanted world.
The deconstruction for me was there in that one place, in that one time,
So brightly illuminated that my eyes were momentarily blinded
And my nostalgic wish was to see His blood, once again, as they had,
Though in my world, at my age, nostalgia is usually wasted,
Awash in the liquidity of post-modernity, metering the harm.
I passed on, though less leisurely and less at ease.

Neither Here Nor There![1]

It isn't there, you know,
And it's not here.
Not everything has a place,
Nothing has a place.
There is a law against that,
Placeness, I mean.
Get out your odds book,
And I can help you
Outline the fuzziness,
The pixilation,
Draw some boundaries,
But not barriers.
Place is over-rated anyway.
It's predictability you really want,
And if life were all predictable,
How boring ….
But don't worry,
Because it and nothing else is there,
It's actually everywhere,
Which doesn't help when you really need it,
Not that you can't have it,
But not have it also,
Even though it is somewhere near your hand!
Think about it,
Until you get used to it,
Then you think you know it,
But it's, in fact, not here!
It's just more familiarly not here!

---

[1] *Originally published in* The Scandalous Lives of Butterflies, *ed. Kevin L. Cole, Scurfpea Publishing, Sioux Falls, 2015.*

On the Job

We are the no-men,
We are the snow-men,
    Melting incognito.
We are the yes-men,
We are less-than-men,
    Choosing that god's caress,

Our backs are corn stobs
Burning in the sun
Under the watchful eyes
Of a frayed black crow.

I spit on ourselves.

Before the Battles

High stiff collar against smooth cheeks,
Polished brass and oiled leather,
Hair combed back like a helmet,
Musket at present,
Collected and ready,
Frozen in time –
As peaceful as war can be.

Richard Lyman Lewis (1844 – 1867), Alabama, CFA, is the great grandfather of the author.

Under the Bomb

6 August 1945, when "Little Boy" grew up,
9 August 1945, when "Fat Man" lost considerable weight.

What does it matter to claim impossibility?[1]
"Thou knowest no man can split the atom."
"… talking moonshine."
"…not the slightest indication…"
Opinion matters less than actuality.[2]
"It worked."
"There was a great fire ring floating …"

---

[1] *The following quotations are, in order, by: John Dalton who originated the modern atomic theory in 1805; Ernest Rutherford who proposed the nuclear model of the atom and made this comment in 1931; Albert Einstein who derived the $E = mc^2$ equation, the basis for nuclear weapons, commenting in 1933.*

[2] *The following quotations are, in order, by: Robert Oppenheimer who was scientific head of the Manhattan Project speaking just after seeing the first successful atomic bomb test in New Mexico 1945; Dr. Shuntaro Hida, Hiroshima resident who survived the bomb in 1945.*

Compulsion to Speak

Naked ape,
Ruthless killer and eater of its own kind,
Featherless biped,
Not to be confused with a plucked chicken,
Manufacturer (*manu factum*),
Inventor of tools that can till and kill,
Perhaps best,
Linguistic hominid,
Homo sapiens sapiens,
Speaker of the house in the house.

There are 6912 distinct human languages cataloged,[1]
But not,
Esperanto …
Or Igpa Atinla …

?4U
Do we need another made-up language?
YGTBKM – of course,
KPC, if nothing else.
But, SFB,
SOL young technologs will invent it.
STW and you'll find 511
On that particular invention.
9, but they may not be able to understand.
It's lacking verbs,
And it's not vocal.
It's young, but getting older.
IOW YBS IYKWIM.
EOM.

---

[1] Ethnologue: Languages of the World, *15th edition*, ed. Raymond G. Gordon, 2009. ISBN-13: 978-1556711596

Dictionary
    ?4U: Here's a question for you.
    YGTBKM: You've got to be kidding me.
    KPC: Keeping parents clueless.
    SFB: Shit for brains.
    SOL: Sooner or later.
    STW: Search the web.
    511: Too much information.
    9: Parents are watching!
    IOW: In other words.
    YBS: You'll be sorry.
    IYKWIM: If you know what I mean.
    EOM: End of message.

https://www.netlingo.com/dictionary/i.php

Damsel in Distress

Drizzle onto the soft forest floor
and downpour on the hard rocks
exchange,
tearing her upside-down.
At the hospital watch,
in the room with the flickering fluorescents,
the machines hiss and pull,
sheets soggy with sweat and fluids,
opportunities for resuscitation disappearing.
Missed street trolleys clang on down the hill –
alarms sound –
as puddles of muddy water ejected
from its path grease its squealing brakes,
loud over the screams.
The rocks glazed with rain repel water into torrents,
though spread thinly onto the plain,
evaporating into salt flats,
not yet reaching the mother water –
the soul is torn away.
Some vagabond escapes,
carried away in the renegade train,
taking no notice of the damage done.

The Top at the Bottom

I went to the toy chest looking for memories,
Recalling the times when young and old mixed so easily.
Their progression is frozen inside the chest –
Candy Land and Alphabet Bingo,
To Monopoly Junior and Uno,
To Clue and Labyrinth.

I can see them growing, shedding dependence –
When Care Bears dominoes were a challenge,
Replaced by playing a decent game of checkers,
And recently elated over a knight fork.

At the bottom among a few escaped Lincoln Logs,
I found my old handmade top, a bit scarred and cracked –
Symbolic, but missing the Hebrew message of a dreidel –
As old as I, but young as ever.
I wrapped its cord and flicked it into motion,
Setting it free to do its thing.
Of course it still works –
More than can be said for the Etch A Sketch
With its permanently etched image,
Or that mini Pac Man, even with new batteries.

The top was never actually played with as a toy,
But it was early and late an object of interest when they spun it.
And why not –
it's moving in one way but strangely not in another?
Even young ones are fascinated by that special kind of independence.

I think I shall keep the top.
Perhaps I would like to think
I too will still work,
Can spin a bit,
And remain something of interest.

Chauvet-Pont-d'Arc[1]

The cave: no doubt a sanctuary,
But also a place of awe and trembling.

Here the mark of human artistic creativity –
A magic that makes the transitory permanent
And captures the spirit outside of the existence.

How profound the visionary
Who took crude tools in hand
And imprinted his vision on the walls,
Revealing the eye of the mind.

That act is worthy of worship,
Sacred because it is the inanimate
That comes alive in the mind of another,
And speaks through time with the artist's voice.
This is reality which is not real – a creation,
A consensual hallucination of reality,
Demanding attention and reverence.

The Cro-Magnon[2] artists would recognize such images now –
Not the meaning, but the use of images.
How imagination puts images into motion
Was all that was required at Chauvet Cave
Thirty millennia ago.

---

[1] *Cave discovered in southern France in 1994 containing some of the finest prehistoric artwork produced by those inhabiting the cave between 28,000 and 37,000 years ago.*

[2] *Cro Magnon is not the proper technical designation of these individuals, but is a commonly used term for the earliest modern humans (Homo sapiens sapiens) in Europe. Current literature refers to them as European Early Modern Humans (EEMH), the first documented of which is a specimen from Southern Italy dated at about 43,000 years BP.*

Visual sophistication in 1895 was more refined,
But those in the audience who saw the Lumière brothers'
L'arrivée d'un train en gare de La Ciotat,[3]
In darkness on a life-size screen,
Ran from the apparition in terror
As the image plowed toward them
In a motion too real for their visual imagination.

Modern image has lost its surprise,
With a sensory-overloaded audience
And its visual content so much busier and more varied,
But perhaps not more sophisticated,
And surely accepted with much less reverence,
Especially if your goal is to anthropomorphize cats,
Assuming *http://www.LOLcats.com/* would suffice as an example.

---

[3] *The Arrival of a Train at La Ciotat Station*

Acetylcholinesterase, I Know Thee Well[1]

Acetylcholinesterase, dear serine hydrolase,
Improbably attentive for one membrane bound,
Waiting patiently for your substrate
In that neuromuscular synapse.

The excitement that comes so naturally down the line
Must in the end be quenched – your job!
Tension builds as it approaches,
Acetylcholine, its quaternary ammonium ion
Gracefully parachuting down the active site cleft,
Gently attaching to those sticky aromatic amino acid residues,
Tryptophan, Phenylalanine, Tyrosine,
Before releasing and continuing the plunge.

Always polite, AChE greets its substrate:
"Welcome to my active site, acetylcholine!
Snap into my complementary dock,
Nestle there next to my catalytic triad –
Bold serine always ready to leap forward and penetrate,
Hot histidine eager to prep its serine,
Cool glutamate hovering to quench histidine's excess."

---

[1] *Acetylcholinesterase is an enzyme, typically bound to the postsynaptic membrane of a neural junction, whose function is to terminate chemically-transmitted nerve signals across a synapse (synaptic transmission) by breaking apart the neurotransmitter acetylcholine. Inhibition of this enzyme by organophosphorus nerve agents (e.g. Sarin gas) or pesticides (e.g. malathion) can easily kill (either a person or some insect pest) through nerve overstimulation.*

Serine, primed and on the attack,
Drives its nucleophilic electron pair
Into the substrate's carbonyl pouch.
Acetylcholine in ecstasy,
Ejects its choline burden
And, slimmed down, snuggles even closer in the cleft.
But, not allowed to relax yet,
A scurrying water molecule,
Leaping through the now open door of the active site,
Pecks away at the exposed carbonyl of the acyl enzyme,
Stripping away the acetate residue from the enzyme's embrace,
Leaving the active site barren and disappointed
But ready to tryst again,
Fickle those lovers are!

So my acetylcholinesterase cycle continues,
Splitting acetylcholines without missing a beat,
Repetitive and boring in its well-evolved metronomic dance,
But calmingly so sure and predictable.

Doors

Doors that open automatically on approach.
Doors that say "Pull" and are pushed.
Doors that revolve, requiring some cooperation for use.
Doors that must remain unlocked during business hours.
Doors that are double and triple locked.
Doors with screens that are open when closed.
Doors that slam shut in your face, literally or figuratively.
Doors of opportunity.
Doors to heaven or hell.
Doors hiding prizes. (Should you change doors?)
Doors with broken hinges and missing knobs.
Doors promising privacy which can be opened with a paperclip.
Doors that are also windows.
Doors that open on Thanksgiving for Christmas shopping.
Doors with bars that segregate.
Doors on cars that close on little fingers without regard.
Doors that spring open to reveal spiders.
Doors that allow or deny access,
Doors of perception, via mescaline in the marriage of heaven and hell, except for,
Doors performing after Jim's death.

In the Coop

She –
As close to a dinosaur as you can get now –
Strides forth haughtily,
Queen of her domain.
Earthy arthropods and nematodes,
Helpless as her mouth descends upon them,
At the top of the pecking order, literally.
Also exemplary mother,
    protector of the nest,
    diligent in attention to her eggs,
    never eating her hatchlings.
But dinosaurhood, once again,
Is in the end no license for longevity,
In the world of grilled, extra crispy, or original.

The Bust of Socrates

I wake in the predawn darkness,
With but a weak shaft of light through the trees onto my window,
And vaguely see the bust of Socrates.
See, touch, hear, taste, smell,
And neural ripples cast the sensory spell,
Patterned networks of neurons activated.
Not a place!
That is reality, as the bust of Socrates is real.
Not *the* reality – a personal reality,
My neural network, at this time,
Not at a place!
No object is more real in any other sense.

Awakening, I imagine Socrates in the agora,
Dusty and sweating and talking and questioning –
Not to see, touch, hear, taste, or smell,
But neural ripples cast the imagery spell,
Patterned networks of neurons activated.
Not a place!
That is the image, as the image of the agora is real.
Not *the* image – a personal image,
My neural network, at this time,
Not at a place!
No image exists more real in any other sense.

Some objects are less real than their images –
A perfect equilateral triangle as an examined object does not exist,
But the image does!
It is the solipsist's dream come true.
Reality or imagination – which is purer?
Doctor Johnson kicked the rock,
But images kick butt in dreams.
Neural networks,
Not a place!
are as close to the reality as you can get.

Perhaps the bust of Socrates as a real object,
Changing minute by minute as illumination in the morning changes,
And my network of activated neurons changing accordingly,
Is no less ephemeral than my image of Socrates in the agora.

Around the Stove, 1945

The hardware store at Park and Broadway displayed a doctor's buggy on the floor,
Long after seeing a buggy or wagon on the street was rare
And autos lined Broadway, especially on Saturdays.
The store used to stock bulk foods – flour, cornmeal, sugar, navy beans –
But as the town grew around it, now just the usual hardware items –
Nails, nuts and bolts, tools, paint, housewares, and the like.
My favorite place in the store was by the counter display from the Ames Knife Co.,
Meticulously maintained by Mr. Dooley, their traveling salesman.
Most items in the store, though new, looked a bit worn and used,
But the knives were shiny and polished with crisp unworn outlines under the glass cover.
Imagining their possibilities kept a young mind endlessly occupied.
The store also stocked a group of older men, mostly farmers,
Who, in the winter months, still congregated around the pot belly stove,
Sitting in old cane bottom chairs or on nail barrels,
Drinking coffee from the chipped blue enamel coffee pot
And holding forth with gossip and general bullshit.
There was a new café in town with bright lights and Formica-topped tables,
But the old crocks preferred a place where they didn't have to scrape the mud off their boots,
And the coffee was free.
A few still farmed using horses and got their tack when needed from the store,
But most were either retired or had a tractor and a few implements suitable for scratch farming.
After harvest, when the harnesses had been mended, tines straightened,
Axel hubs packed, broken wheels welded, and all was in readiness for the winter,
They once again became regulars at the store.
Silhouetted around the stove,
They seemed like tombstones, speaking their epitaphs –
Perhaps no less ephemeral that the chiseled kind which no one bothers to read
After their family is dead or moved away –
They, like the store and the stones, holding on to the familiar for a while longer
Before inevitable erosion with the passing years.

'Possum Hunt, 1927

They trailed down the road a bit in complete darkness,
Until the music from the jive joint at Clark's Corner faded,
Before the dogs were unleashed.
The moonless night was fall dry, windless, and still hot,
Making the chase a simple task.

They knew the dogs had treed the 'possum,
By the change in Homer's howl.
The pack consisted of that bluetick hound, the nose,
And "Dog," grandpa's brutish Rottweiler, the muscle –
With a particular dislike for 'possums.

The men crashed through the brush and found the dogs.
At a husky sixteen years,
Dad was carrying the heavy electric lamp,
And a few others were carrying coal oil lanterns.
"Light 'em up" grandpa said.
The 'possum was high up,
eyes reflecting in the electric beam.

Grandpa's single shot .410, light-loaded with BBs,
immediately cracked,
Echoing through the woods over Homer's racket.
Grandpa doesn't miss, but the 'possum didn't fall,
Which was the intended outcome –
Warning given, order re-established.

The lamp was switched off, dogs leashed,
And the group made its way back to the road.
Near the road Grandpa told Dad
to gather a few ripe persimmons –
Nothing better than Grandma's
persimmon pudding with roasted pecans,
After a night in the woods.

It's Just for You

*Aquilegia canadensis (*Canadian Columbine*)*
*Flowers red to yellow, usually 3 – 4 cm long. Spurs much
longer than the blades of the petals. plants with stems 3 –
9 dm tall, with compound leaves, the ultimate segments
with rounded, crenate teeth. Flowers few, large and showy,
solitary at the ends of branches. Friuts of 5 follicles, loosely
connivent at maturity. Infrequent on loamy, woody hillsides
…. Apr – May. – Theodore Van Bruggen[1]*

I have a small field of columbines
a five-dove cluster some see
eagle-taloned vulgar cultivar[2]
spikey yet yearning flower
in the hands of the garden miners
displaced from natives of cool northeastern
deciduous forest remnants in Dakota
when in bloom a lavender wave floating
over ugly olive-drab greenery
self-seeded and bird-planted
in my former tomato patch
shaded out by the green ash tree
still suffering ice storm woes
sitting in a green plastic Adirondack chair
under the ash watching the lavender wave
why does it make me think of *Carmina Burana*[3]
Benedictine juvenilia gone mad with boredom

> *a spring flower, merry face of spring*
> *laughing on joyous cool woody slopes*
> *the promise of a thousand joys*

---

[1]*Van Bruggen, Theodore.* The Vascular Plants of South Dakota, *Iowa State University Press, Ames, 1976, page 219*

[2]Aquilegia x hybrid *most likely with* Aquilegia vulgaris *having variable flower color.*

[3]*The italicized stanzas in the following are my attempts to capture a condensed essence of the message in the much larger presentation of Carmina Burana.*

> *spring's power bids us to rejoice*
> *winter sadness is now at an end*

like the seductive promise from a lover

> *sweet rose-red lips*
> *come and make me better*

but *O Fortuna* the spring crispness of the unspoiled blossom

> *waxing only promising waning*
> *power and poverty*
> *the spring fades away like ice*
> *fate strikes down even the stronger*
> *everyone shall weep for the flower*

what then is left unknown in my green chair
that columbine is a false prophet
but I might hold onto the promise

> *I am eager for the pleasures of spring flesh*
> *and those sweet rose-red lips*
> *more than for salvation*
> *if my soul is departed*
> *so I shall attend to the carnal*

all for the pleasure of a flower
that virgin lavender undulation so brief
a profound responsibility for one so fragile
I suppose

Austin, 1972

The two waitresses in the campus eatery
Are braless – Welcome to Austin!
One wears a tank top, suitably stretched,
The other a more modest shirt,
But silhouetted against any light …
Little is left to imagination,
But imagination is far from exhausted.

My summer postdoc at UT,
An unexpected beginning for one
Accustomed to more prudish surroundings
Where such publicly visible breasts
Inhabited only titty bars.
For naked apes,
Wearing your ass on your chest
Is an excellent advertising strategy,
But I was not a consumer
Of either the sexual or emancipation statements,
And only inadvertently an observer –
Though not a hostile one.

Curiously at the end of my ten-week stint in Austin,
My return to river city found my wife,
Not encased in plastic wrap
Or any other exotic come-on.
But braless in a new knit sweater
With a low swooping bodice –
Welcome Home!
Hooray for the transmission speed
Of cultural evolution.

Lost in Translation

My pen speaks for my brain,
In awkward angled lines on inexhaustible sheets.
My pen speaks to
    amuse,
    annoy,
    berate,
    provoke,
    educate,
    pontificate
    …
My brain broadcasts at 20 Mbs,
My pen speaks at 1 bs,
A discontinuity intolerable.
My brain skips arhythmically,
My pen pauses untranslatably,
A thought is abandoned or perverted,
Perhaps an important infinitesimal.
My brain knows but cannot express.
My pen hangs suspended –
What mental recess needs interrogation?
On the endless paper,
Pen speak is far from brain speak –
There is emptiness in the difference.
What "I" want to say
Is not spoken by either.

Avatar

The avatar resides on my bookshelf
In no particular privileged location.
She is dressed in formal, native Chinese attire,
Cantonese, I believe,
Which has a Japanese flavor,
Especially with the hair ornament style.
She watches me silently,
And perhaps a bit judgmentally,
But abandonly hopeful, or so I interpret.
She has been my companion for many years,
Given to me by the woman she represents –
Talented and desirable, but ever unattainable.

Why do I not discard her?
I suppose because she worked –
Her voodoo magic, or the oriental equivalent,
Entrapped part of me,
In that magic memory of attraction,
When such memories are so rare,
Even their residue holds some power.
Not speaking of carnality or raw desire,
But of both spoken and unspoken communion –

A comfortable and effortless blending of spirit and purpose,
Which represents a kind of intellectual lust for attachment –
The Kierkegaardian conundrum.
And do you really discard even a casual avatar friend
For no compelling reason?

But there is a social standard that quantizes relationships –
Choices must be made,
Freedoms restricted.
My allowed states are and were filled,
Perhaps still to the regret of my silent friend.
Yet the steadfast avatar retains an aura of unfaithfulness
That accompanies her physical presence.
One need not be conventionally religious
To appreciate the instruction that
"Lust in heart" is sin equivalent to "lust in hand."
Thus conflicted, the avatar remains on my shelf,
A fading memory, yet resisting abandonment.

From the Candle's Perspective[1]

A candle lit *in memorium*
Has an agenda of its own.

The undulating flame outlined
With tiny incandescent carbonaceous soot particles,
Electrons pulsing wildly,
Converting paraffin chemical energy to light and heat radiation.
O_2, the breath of plants, sacrificed,
CO_2 and H_2O, transparent gases,
Spiral upwards out of the flame,
Mimicking the outflow of cellular respiration –
My breath is like the breath of a candle.
Atmospheric CO_2 ticks upward,
With global warming consequences.
The carbon soot, cooled and condensed,
Holds microscopic sparkly diamond crystals
And fragments of greasy-gray graphite,
But also a few delightfully independent carbon balls,
Geodesic cages of exactly sixty carbon atoms,
Buckminsterfullerene –
formal name quirkiness not often encountered –
A ruby surprise from an old element.
The burning candle is changed in one sense,
But every carbon, hydrogen, oxygen atom engaged
Is accounted for exactly in the products
And not changed in that sense –
Candle and oxygen consumed, but not gone.

A candle lit symbolically
Has an actuality –
Different worlds worthy of notice.

---

[1] *Encomium to Michael Faraday's* Six Royal Institution Lectures, *"The Chemical History of a Candle," presented in 1848.*

Apart-ment

The older woman who drives the yellow Chevette
uses the back stairs and is seldom seen.
The young woman above my rooms
entertains guys a lot, sometimes noisily.
Two black dudes across the hall,
good-natured, with much coming and going.
Friday and Saturday nights, that heavy, sweet aroma settles in,
comforting in its insouciance.
A tenuous and somewhat strange family for sure,
but there is a connection here,
if just for a enough time to feel it.

The Girl in the Green Dress

The girl in the long, flowing green dress
Floated into my classroom
Accompanied by her dog,
Foursquarely attached to the ground.

She took a seat on the aisle
And her companion folded up beside her, chin on paws,
But ears erect and eyes watchful,
His long collie nose examining the room.

Idly, she dropped her hand to touch his head.
Her aura settled over the sparsely-populated room,
New arrivals sinking silently into seats,
Somehow compelled to complacency.

I approached the pair casually,
Tracked purposefully by large brown eyes,
But without any nervous reaction.
I glimpsed the toes of her sandals,

Under the hem of her long, flowing green dress.
She had a psychology text on her desk,
So I said, "Psychology is P–S-Y, but this is a Physics, P-H-Y, class."
She looked up – eyes just as brown and moist –

"I know, but he came in here, so Physics it is."
Interestingly, her nonjudgmental response relaxed my tension
And I made no comment about the obvious.
Thus the class began and continued

In her aura with the silent dog – day after day
Through the hot physics summer –
A naïve elegance,
Sophistication in simplicity of demeanor,

And unspoken communication between the pair,
That somehow propelled the class.
And so it was for the summer term,
A relaxed immersion in physics,

With me, the teacher, also receiving instruction.
They never missed a day,
But leaving class that last day of the summer session,
The silent partner exited and barked – once.

And "they" got an "A" for the class.
Later I checked on these summer students,
Mine was the only course they ever took.
I wonder, is my planned life any less random?

Visit to Good Earth State Park at Blood Run[1]

I.
He heard them in the rustle high in the oaks,
And mingled with the murmur of the river far below,
In the woody silence, quiet voices of the clans.
The deer were not trespassers,
The child's grave was not a trespasser,
He was the trespasser, though he trod lightly.
A thousand whispers, a thousand years old –
In the rustle and murmur,
In the poised deer and the silent grave –
Condemned him.
Humbly, with eyes averted,
He withdrew.

II.
Deer are safe in the park,
with predators, human and otherwise, absent or disarmed.
Their trail through the woods is well-defined
along the steep bluff above the river –
a path I too follow, treading lightly as possible.

Deer insouciantly melt away,
rather than face a direct encounter,
but when I sit back to a tree near the trail,
I might as well be a cow –
my scent is not registered foreign,
no danger to deer as they pass, browsing contentedly.

---

[1] *South Dakota state park located along the Big Sioux River, southeast of Sioux Falls. The site was a meeting place and cultural center for many tribes of the Oneota Indigenous Peoples between 1300 and 1700 CE. The park provided a more peaceful respite prior to the construction of a visitor center and observation platforms hanging over the bluffs.*

Near the park boundary the bluff descends
to river level and a possible deer crossing,
which can be viewed from a bluff overhang.
The river is lethargic in the high summer and the fall,
perilous as the water cascades in the spring,
yet necessary passage all year as the quickest way in and out.

At middle stream, a sand island emerges in low water,
becoming an immersed sand shoal in spring,
but the deer evidently mark its hidden location.
I saw a crossing deer pause to rest there as on stilts,
high water dividing around her thin legs,
eyes wary, ears erect and mobile,
as she scanned the opposite shore, beyond the safe park.

Once, later in the season, I met a deer emerging on the far side.
Now I was immediately sensed as threat,
no longer just a cow to be tolerated,
and she bolted into a thicket with that flash of white.
I never see deer ambling through the woods across the river,
as they know I am to be avoided on that shore –
I am man, perhaps with different pheromones,
unworthy of trust in new circumstances,
though my intentions had not consciously changed.

Deer keep neither hardcopy records nor history –
their knowledge is their life
built by their environment into behavior.
Yet by their actions they tell,
not only of their own kind of innate intelligence,
but a revelatory tale about beings such as myself.

No Remorse in Wyoming

I.
He shot the encroaching stranger,
purposefully and with deadly intent.
That's what NO TRESPASSING means!

II.
"Nothing for you – get away from my door,"
he told the scraggly man.
Later he found the dead man inconveniently huddled next to his porch.

III.
The casino ad and the UNICEF plea arrived in his email.
He lost his $1000 tax refund at the casino.
Children died, so he heard.

In Our Image

That old God won't do –
Too much baggage, too much authority.
But we're culturally determined to need one,
Yet any appeal to authority
Is so compromising
As a logical fallacy.
We need understanding of situational ethics:
God-like, but
Semi-God – just on Sunday, 11:00 – 12:00,
Pseudo-God – just gives timeouts,
God-lite – the low sin alternative,
God-ette,
God-ish,
God-oid,
God-ot,
attending to some of our needs, eventually.

Better Things for Better Living…
Through Chemistry

The cut-down Siberian elm refused my offer to die gracefully,
year-after-year lifting to heaven
its leafy arms out of the ground.

Finally, poisoned, the I-killed-thee tree expired ungracefully,
oozing toxins from the tips of its finest roots
all the way to the margins of its former drop zone,
exudates, in their underground manner,
surreptitiously killing all they touched –
revenge extracted.

I tell those curious about the dead zone,
arcing with semi-circular precision across my lawn,
that it must be an urban crop circle – seriously!

Springtime Not Really So Bad Blues

Rabbit ate my tulips.
Rabbit chewed the bark of my barberry bush.
Rabbit ate my newly-planted Roma tomato.
Rabbit ate the apple slice – in my live trap.
Rabbit eats clover,
Down by the river.

Squirrel showered the lawn with branches of my green ash tree.
Squirrel ate the sunflower seeds in my bird feeder, scattering the rest.
Squirrel incisored the seats of my picnic table.
Squirrel ate the peanuts – in my live trap.
Squirrel eats last years' walnuts,
Down by the river.

Granddaughter broke the door of my CD player.
Granddaughter lost the Queen of Spades from my deck.
Granddaughter got grape jam on my favorite chair.
Granddaughter watches rabbit and squirrel,
Down by the river –
As she eats the ice cream cone I bought her.

Grandpa gets older, Granddaughter,
So that you can grow up!
When you get all grown up,
Grandpa will no longer need worry,
About rabbits and squirrels.

An Icy Winter's Tale

Out of the swarm, a lazy few stuck,
Relaxing in their special places, mollified.
They, pioneers in a sense, set the concretion in motion,
Partners holding hands rapturously entwined,
Entering the nebular spiral of condensation,
Settling carefully into that exergonic minimum.
Now microscopic with fractal repeat, the shape emerges,
En route to a macroscopic crystalline entity,
That hexagonal lattice of near infinite diversity,
Yet held honest to those natural symmetry demands –
Joined by chance, but compelled by necessity,
Into a proper visible function of the invisible.
Finally it fell, languidly dissolving on my tongue,
Tasteless, but highly nutritious in concept and deed.

Return to Old Haunts[1]
by Steve Boint

Wish I knew where the poets have gone.
Stock quotes. Zoning issues.
Inspirational management books.
No Nietzsche. No Rand. No Hegel.

The grass is dead
but littered with greenbacks.

I'd settle for a scientist
or an artist.

The following was written in response by Lewis:

Where are the Poets?[2]

Trampled by the Hegelian mechanical march –
we are just that we were?
Subsumed by the *Übermenschen* of the 0.1% –
valueless, unmeasured in dollars?
Rejected by the Randian I, I, I, … –
empathy ground to dust by ego?

I dream the uncertainty of the poem,
the tolerance of the measurement,
the possibility from the eyes of another.

---

[1] *Originally published in*, Boint, Steve. Physicist at the Window, *Scurfpea Publishing, Sioux Falls, 2014. Copyright © Steve Boint, 2014. All rights reserved.*
[2] *Revised version from that published in* The Scandalous Lives of Butterflies, *ed. Kevin L. Cole, Scurfpea Publishing, Sioux Falls, 2015.*

Just in Time

Our time is familiarly running out,
provisionally finite,
like water evaporating in a perpetual drought,
with no rainfall to recover.

Time, so familiar, as the fourth dimension,
yet so strange,
begging the question
of how many dimensions are sufficient to describe our world.

Time and disorder arrow each other,
slowing or accelerating,
in fact or metaphor,
but never ceasing or reversing.

Those interesting fictions – of Dorian, Benjamin, and Bill –
tempt us to believe the impossible about life and time,
in harmless programmed fantasy,
or imagining the finger of an Augustinian God writing the stories.

This God of Augustine was,
outside of time, created time, exists at all points in time,
but Augustine had a vivid imagination –
as if words might construct the world.

The aura of Augustine's God ensures
you cannot win,
you cannot break even,
you must play the game!

Personal time is running out – God or not –
with the inexorable shortening of telomeres,
the mainspring's increasing slackness in our clockwork existence,
where all are equal under entropy's eye and time's arrow.

Perhaps rational insanity is a cure –
blessed immolation in a dimension otherwise unknown,
a timelessness imposed internally in an imagined infinity,
as synaptic storms rage:

skip ye merrily through the meadows,
roam in magic lands unknown,
explore the endless seas – plus ultra –
all reality expunged in eternal dreams,
and time denied in solipsistic bliss,
disorder redefined as order,
where turning back hands turns back time.

Such heaven in mind becomes a hope fulfilled,
though a ritual, thought-numbing suicide –
a hard choice that, but the only out,
if out is a choice in this one-way world.

But mercifully,
my background hum always interrupts,
rejecting insanity for pain –
just in time.

That Included Middle[1]

"It was the best of times, it was the worst of times…"
heralds a good story, not nonsense.
Look around the consensual hallucination of the Internet,
talk around the complex web of social media,
think around the acceleration of choice –
truth and untruth are equal in time,
"X" and "⌐X" simultaneously,
is not meaningfully illogical,
∴ "God" and "⌐God" are both Great Truths,[2]
as Love and Hate
are not irreconcilable emotional states
on the stage of this used world,
where formal logic is illogical,
with Gödel's laugh echoing in the Cloud:

---

[1] The "law of excluded middle" is one of the classic laws of logical thought. It states that for any proposition, either that proposition is true, or its negation is true; that is, there is no possible middle ground between the two parts of a contradiction. The quotation in the first line is from A Tale of Two Cities by Charles Dickens.

[2] "The opposite of a great truth is also true." – Niels Bohr, The Philosophical Writings of Niels Bohr

From the language tumbles,
among the definition stumbles,
one truth, and truth is perverted,
singular truth is converted,
but no one truth is deserted,
truth is that which is asserted –

a deflating nightmare to philosophers
when "nothing is true" and "everything is true,"[3]
are equally valid,
where only descriptive categories,
minority and majority views exist –
I might just as well be that poached egg – [4]
though, long term, natural selection does weigh in,
much to the chagrin of those so constrained by rules.

---

[3] *Well, what Gödel actually says is that some things are "true" but "unprovable." Good luck on getting that across.*

[4] *Referring to Bertrand Russell's famous line disparaging radical skepticism: "The lunatic who believes that he is a poached egg is to be condemned solely on the ground he is in the minority...."* Russell, Bertrand. A History of Western Philosophy, *Book-of-the-Month Club edition, New York, 1995, p. 673.*

Truth Said

Evidence presented and rebutted,
Objections noted,
Reasonable doubt weighed,
Verdict rendered,
Judicial truth said.
New evidence: suspect exonerated,
Wrongful conviction lawsuit filed.

Sacred texts studied,
Interpretations rendered,
Foes demonized,
Orthodoxy introduced,
Revealed truth said.
Social change: hermeneutical fine-tuning,
Same people in charge.

Candidates declare,
Options explained,
Much money spent,
Voters vote,
Political truth said.
Economy tanks: politicians sacrificed,
Rich get richer.

Opponents granted an audience,
Briefs filed, oral arguments heard,
Advocates questioned showily,
5 – 4 decision rendered,
Constitutional truth said.
Meanings of words change: precedent overthrown,
Either the left or right incensed.

Observations and data obtained,
Theories proposed and tested,
Falsification narrows field,
Consensus probability level established,
Scientific truth said.
Better measurements: new theory constructed,
Nobel Prize awarded.

Lines written,
Sensible or not,
Reread or not,
Published or not,
Poetic truth said.
"Truth" just as easily false as true:
But it really doesn't matter that much.

On the Cusp of a Poem

To enthrall, but haunt –

Whitman had his flesh, Rich her power,
Dickinson her secrets, and Oliver her land.
You have only random ghosts of ideas,
passing transparently, admitting to no shadows.

That momentary insight or single vision,
some speck in the dust cloud,
flickers past as a bare seed,
one frame of unknown origin and unrealized potential –

Leaving you, the puzzled gardener,
to create a memory of vegetative flux,
grasping to ensoil and vitalize the embryo,
so quickly being swept away with the chaos.

On a Rubber Duck

That day long past,
    when dirt roads existed
    and led somewhere
    besides up to the house on the hill,
And kids in short and long pants
Kicked the sawdust on circus tent floors –
    chocolate double scoops
    that melted too soon in the carnival heat
    and trailed sugary brown rivulets.
That spring, summertime
    with clattering lawnmowers
    and a galloping jiffy broom,
With twilight smells
Spread out like a patchwork quilt on the evening breeze.
The sight, the sound –
    glow worms in quart Mason jars
    on the dresser covered
    now and then by those filmy curtains
    in the moving airs
    that must be alive.
But a rubber duck, that once was alive
In a bathtub, sudsy domain,
Stares silently across the years from a shelf.
That time,
That age,
Was too simple ever to have existed.

To My Attention

The sun is low,
its light strained into an orange lollipop.
My sky is high,
though not mine alone
as, in the darkening, F-16s are doing touch-and-goes,
riding on steaks of fire
in intimate practice for practical wars,
whether they dodge drones or not,
tiny specks below radar.

Why watch those when I could be
watching the woman across the street
unwittingly illuminated on her mundane stage,
undangerously working at kitchen tasks?

The international space station,
which I had turned out to see,
streaks in from the northwest –
a sparkle declaring itself the brightest star
among the contrails, yet peacefully
out of reach of noise and threat from F-16s –
disappearing rainbow-like
below the tree line in the southeast
as if in a hurry to another task.
I add a Marvel swoosh in its wake
and think about naming it Superhero ISSy.

I'm here in the ambivalence of a too golden crepuscule,
reconciled to the vagaries of the evening
where the commonplace hardly registers
and the good things pass by silently.
Sadly I can only attend to the shrieks.

Nietzsche Simplified

325K *76K* *26K*

Weep for Nietzsche – Fritz I know thee well –
shy, unaffected, with mustache mask,
penurious, polite to a fault,
sojourner German philologist,
for all time most unlike the image –
no *Zarathustra*, no *Übermensch*,

no left-wing revolutionary,
no anti-Semite proto-Nazi,
antichristian, not the Antichrist –
bereft emotional attachment,
living nomad-like in boarding rooms
across the Swiss and Italian Alps.

Eating, an agony of choices,
for every simple menu mistake –
tea too strong, food too spicy or rich –
a too sensitive stomach rebels,
and sets off those piercing headaches that
drive spikes into his concentration.

No wine, beer, coffee, or tobacco –
nothing that excites or relaxes,
just a meager meal humbly alone,
perhaps a harmless conversation
with a compliant fellow boarder,
polite but cursory and brief,

fearing to discuss the death of God,
herds and masters as categories,
that facts melt into interpretations
and truth exists only in a mind.
Then on to a cold, upper chamber –
table and chair, bed, and steamer trunk,

containing his threadbare, modest clothes.
On that table lies his *raison d'être* –
a revisioning of the world on
densely-scribbled sheets, hand writing
indecipherable but to a few,
either as a joke or nightmare.

This stark chamber has no adornment
to relieve either the shabbiness
of his existence or detract from
the philosophical poetry.
Poised menacingly next to his work,
a tray of glass vials containing

myriad medicinal potions –
perhaps better described as poisons –
for treating stomach cramps and migraines
and his incessant insomnia,
inducing unnatural, brief sleep.
In winter, in his unheated room,

bundled in overcoat and wool scarf,
head two inches above the paper,
thick lenses fighting his failing sight,
fingers freezing, but writing for hours,
page after page in his pinched tight script,
words once written he could not re-read.

The Greeks offer a word, *arête*,
which might be translated as "virtue,"
but which has deeper meaning than that –
perhaps a whole-life task devotion,
and here Nietzsche's *arête* appeared
against all opposition to his goal –

lost love, few friends, no relationships,
poverty, missing recognition
of his philosophical impact –
just his ideas, page after page.
Nietzsche's Godfather moment arrived,
awakening with a marble bust

of Dionysus between his legs,
recognition screaming through his works
as that marble weight crushed him between
Athenian values and morals
and being the good European.
Weep then as you would for Œdipus,

Nietzsche's self-proclaimed *Doppelgänger*,
fellow traveler, the last human,
serving as existentialist image
of *Wissenshaft* as Œdipus/Sphinx,
with humans the source of both questions
and answers on the human contract.

He queries, "Which…is the Œdipus here?
Which the Sphinx?" in this dangerous game
where risk is merely asking questions
and then being willing to accept
responsibility for answers.
Blind Œdipus and insane Nietzsche

stand as silent warnings for choosing
the vagaries of the questing life,
whether inside or outside of the laboratory.
Nietzsche/Œdipus/Sphinx – one is real –
some multiple personality
disorder from the tragedies birth,

or his *corpus callosum* was jammed,
right brain speaking apart from left brain,
best interpreted as poetry.
We know those voices and harmonies,
those ghosts with whom we communicate –
mere musings to Jekyll/Hyde ogres.

Œdipus is a voice not often
heard by scientists contemplating
passion and pain only in the quest
to answering the riddle, slighting
inevitable consequences,
a disappearance of the human,

"…the last human being in the universe:
the last sigh, your sigh, dies with me…."[1]
Œdipal/Sphinx Nietzsche cohabits

---

[1] *From a fragment of what Nietzsche called "History of Posterity," translated by David Krell and Donald Bates in* The Good European, *University of Chicago Press, 1997, p. 84.*

with Nietzsche torn between Apollo
and the *Dithyrambs of Dionysus*[2] –
order and certainty contrasted

with impulse and intoxicated
risk-taking, as the Greeks would put it –
assume the answers and rules are there,
but the inventive path is not fixed.
Nietzsche is stuck in a very real
Apollonian/Dionysian

conundrum with all the scientists.
His Dionysian "God is dead,"
a shot positing the humanist
requirement for Apollonian
interpretations establishing
the facts of human experience

and truths of human social order,
but destroying previous regimes.
Deconstructing roads between Athens
and Jerusalem risks chaos at best,
a Dionysian task with no
certain Apollonian endgame.

Nietzsche, the last human, took the risk,
betting on the lyre of Apollo.
Intoxicating, Nietzsche can be,
whether one is intoxicated
with his evil spirit constructed
as he lay insane for a decade

---

[2]*Dithyrambs of Dionysus was originally published the same year as* Zarathustra, *and the best way I can describe it would be as a good model for Ginsburg's "Howl." A dithyramb is a song to Dionysus. See,* Dithyrambs of Dionysus, *Bilingual Edition. R. J. Hollingdale, trans., Anvil Press Poetry, London, 2001.*

or with the cardboard movie idol
interpreted from his poetry.
Those acolytes trooping through the Alps,
literally tracing his footsteps –
Spaziergänge durch Nietzsche's Raum³ –
are wandering in their own shadows.

Nietzsche was Œdipus and Sphinx –
interrogating that synthesis
leads to darkness not enlightenment.
Looking for Nietzsche's experience
is a negation of one's own worth –
a hellish eternal recurrence.

Nietzsche cannot serve as blueprint,
rather, it is *he* who recreates,
and from that recognition can come
the intoxication of insight –
play a little, like the good human
adolescents we must surely be,

and make fun of our predicament,
struggling for comprehension on our
quixotic path to discovery.
But be warned, when Nietzsche gives insight,
just as the Sphinx did for Œdipus,
he takes something vital from us –

---

[3] *Translated as "strolls through Nietzsche's area." There is an actual book, Raabe, Paul,* Spaziergänge durch Nietzsche's Sils-Maria. ISBN: *9783716021828.*

Nietzsche, the subterranean voice,
as underground existentialist,
just like Dostoevsky and Dylan,
is a mole into our consciousness.
When we "use" a *part* of this Nietzsche,
we are finally left with his curse,

"The worst readers are those who proceed
like plundering warriors – they pick
up the few things they can use, soil and
confuse the rest and blaspheme the whole,"[4]
exempli gratia, caging Nietzsche in
little programmed, tight boxes herewith.

Uncertain whether slave or master,
uncertain who is really insane,
Nietzsche or ourselves, we are left with
the final echo of his stoic roots,
those words he must have used in dark times,
all his fates assured, *"Amor fati!"*[5]

---

[4] *Nietzsche, Friedrich.* On the Genealogy of Morals, *translated by Walter Kaufman and R. J. Hollingdale, and* Ecce Homo, *translated by Walter Kaufman, Vintage Books, New York, 1967 (Appendix to GOM: Seventy-five Aphorisms from Five Volumes, #137, page 175.)*

[5] *"Love of fate." Nietzsche says, "My formula for greatness in a human being is* amor fati: *that one wants nothing to be different, not forward, not backward, not in all eternity. Not merely bear what is necessary, still less conceal it – all idealism is mendacity in the face of what is necessary – but love it."* Ecce Homo, *Thomas Wayne, trans., Algora Publishing, New York, 2001, p. 39.*

Earth Prayer

*Psoralea esculenta (*Scurfpea*)*

"Stems densely hairy, usually not over 3 dm tall. Leaves principally at the lower part of the stem, their leaflets gray-strigose on the undersurfaces. Flowers in dense cylindric spikes 2 – 8 cm long. Fruiting pods becoming 2 cm long, ovoid and beaked, with strignose hairs. Common in native prairies over the state. May – June."
  —*Theodore Van Bruggen*[1]

Food for the body,
Food for the soul.
If number of names tracks importance,
Psoralea esculenta is prominent:
Prairie turnip, Indian breadroot, scurfpea, prairie potato, tipsin, *pomme blanche, timpsula* ….

Gathering their *timpsula,*
Lakota children thought finding it a game,
But they ate its starchy roots for life.
June is to the Lakota, *tinpsila itkahca wi,*
The moon when breadroot is ripe,
Making their spiritual connection between the heavens and earth.

In 1822 Hugh Glass,
After mauling by grizzly
And abandonment by comrades,
Famously crawled across the prairie to a refuge on the Missouri,
Eating breadroot, his *pomme de terre,* for sustenance,
While dying tissue in his wounds was being eaten,
By maggots –
The merger of living man with living nature.

---

[1]Van Bruggen, Theodore. The Vascular Plants of South Dakota, *Iowa State University Press, Ames, 1976, page 289*

Timsula fades in time, like its language,
Plowed up with the prairie.
Yet symbolically the modest scurfpea may thrive –
As it replenishes the soil with nitrogen, in fact,

It may now replenish our soul,
Offering a bridge between the soul of the earth,
And human use of the earth,
Connecting the Lakota, Hugh Glass, and ourselves.

My fragile scurfpea,
may your message to us persist,
a prayer from the earth to us,
reminding us who must be sustained.

Whence *The Soul of the Rose*[1]

That fragrant and soulful flower,
whose sweet scent is its identity,
famously is what it is —
a translatable soul,
an attraction for the soul-starved,
or the sensual caress to the soul-shocked,
a soul-secret sought by a damaged soul,
but an attractant for bees,
and soul-scent secreted by bees
to mark nectar-rich blossoms,
making it a real thing,
a made thing,
not a supposed thing.
The soulful dance of molecules,[2]

twisting and merging to the scent
that convinces the blind
that it is what it is.
The oil — not in the scent of the oil —
the geraniol — yes, in the scent of the -ol —
the flower itself,
speaking the esoteric chemical language
obeyed as soul-work,
all make the soul-show real.

---

[1] John William Waterhouse, 1908, oil on canvas, 34¾ x 23¼ in. Currently in a private collection. Sold in 2007 for £1,140,000. Image from Wikiart Public Domain.

[2] Magnard, Jean-Louis, et al. "Biosynthesis of monoterpene scent compounds in roses." Science, Vol. 349 no. 6243 pp. 81-83, 3 July 2015. RhNUDX1 is the crucial enzyme in the sequence for the synthesis of the primary "rose" scent, geraniol.

The Scandalous Lives of Butterflies[1]

Asclepias tuberosa (Butterfly Weed)

"*Principal leaves at the middle of the stem alternate. Flowers yellow to bright orange. Stem densely hairy, lacking milky juice. Plants 3 – 6 dm tall, stems several from a deep taproot. Leaves 5 – 10 cm long, linear to lanceolate. Inflorescence of 1 – several umbels, the petals 7 – 10 mm long. Fruiting follicles 7 – 11 cm long, erect. Infrequent in mesic prairie and meadows in the eastern part. June – July.*"
— *Theodore Van Bruggen*[2]

They display a stained-glass coolness,
and by their arrival,
stir a paschal promise of renewal –
lowly worm metamorphosed
to sublime, ethereal being.

Yet by their *Asclepian* heritage,
a bitter, toxic principle[3] is derived,
transparent beneath their beauty
until consumed,
revealing their true, subversive promise –
toxic worm to toxic ethereal being.

As symbol of renewal writ large,
that surface attraction remains,
with the toxic sin latent,
as a Nietzschean Trojan horse,
at its core.
Sample with caution!

---

[1] *Thanks to Matt Dornweiler for the title line. See his poem in* The Scandalous Lives of Butterflies, *ed. Kevin L. Cole, Scurfpea Publishing, Sioux Falls, 2015.*

[2] *Van Bruggen, Theodore.* The Vascular Plants of South Dakota, *Iowa State University Press, Ames, 1976, page 351*

[3] *The secondary metabolites in* Asclepias *are cardiac glycosides which inhibit the Na^+/K^+ ATPase of mammals and birds and discourage consumption.*

A Bowl of Eggs

Near Sacred Heart Mission, rural Pottawatomie County, OK, early spring, 1935. The story goes that after bad times made supporting the whole family on the homestead difficult, Grandpa and Grandma packed the old Buick touring car and headed west to join the Neal cousins who owned a store in central California, leaving the emaciated stock and the hardware store key with Uncle Nels. Grandma said they drove west all day before Grandpa pulled over just across the Texas border, got out and paced back and forth for a long time, cursed God, then turned the car around and headed back home. Grandma said 1936 was a better year. – L. C. Lewis

Each day Grandma filled a small glass bowl with eggs.
Outside with Dust Bowl days unrelenting,
Grandma's enterprising flock of chickens
scavenged those enterprising crawly things
in an otherwise bleak and unrewarding landscape,
returning their daily "nest egg" for the bowl.

German shorthairs, Doc and Rip, monitored the flock,
not particularly fond of the fowl, I'm told,
and unsure of their place in the pecking order,
yet recognizing the peckers as part of the family
and as an extension of Grandma's realm
which they were innately drawn to protect.

1936 (Rural Pottawatomie County, OK): Rip (on the right) and his son, Doc

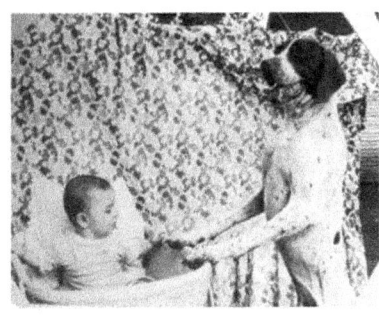

1941: Doc (on the right) and the author at age 8 months

I first remember this land, more verdant and tolerant,
a decade or so later just after the War
but still prowled by the resourceful flock
whose eggs I early learned to gather and protect.
I know Doc and Rip only from old photos,
though I'm told Doc pointed me just like a chicken.

In my time a bowl of eggs still centered the kitchen table.
Though I was not around experiencing the Dust Bowl woes,
I soon learned of Grandma's redemptive symbol,
a focus of continuity and security in those hard times
and a promise of hope and rebirth of better times –
a big responsibility, I suppose, for a simple bowl of eggs.

Author's Comments on the Poetic Impulse

Ursula Le Guin, one of my favorite authors, died early this year leaving this advice to prospective writers: "Write what you know, but remember you may know dragons." After fifty years of doing chemistry research and teaching chemistry to college students, I know a good bit of chemistry; upon retiring and writing my first poetry in 2014 – some of which is attached – I find that I also know dragons. There are a few chemistry elements to my poetry, but being a chemist was my job, not who I am. Some of my dragons come from growing up in south central Oklahoma, a part of the state known locally as "Little Dixie." My maternal grandfather was a member of the revitalized KKK in the 1920's and I heard and understood the stories. My society was highly segregated, and the first time I sat in a classroom with a black person was as a freshman at the University of Oklahoma in 1959. I was attracted to the civil rights movement and, in the middle to late sixties, the Vietnam war protests, both of which freed dragons. My wife and I married in 1968, and we came to Sioux Falls in 1969 where I taught in the chemistry department and in the liberal arts honors program and conducted chemistry research at the University of Sioux Falls. As a teacher and active observer of human behavior, identifying and classifying dragons was an essential part of my life, and flavors my work. The last poetic motivator I will mention comes from my young daughter who asked me a simple question one late summer evening while we were walking the bike trail many years ago: "What is this flower?" I could not answer her very reasonable question. (Later I identified it as a Missouri goldenrod.) Thus began a project to identify and photograph South Dakota wildflowers, a remedy for my ignorance and, as it turned out, a formal excuse to prowl the prairies and woods, both as a solitary and communal exercise. Many years and thousands of photographs later, to my surprise, I found there are both dragons and fairies out there lurking among the forbs and grasses. Some of both show up in my poems.